# Spiritual Jurisdiction

*Mark Bishop*

**Mark Bishop Ministries**
Panama City Beach, Florida

*Spiritual Jurisdiction*
ISBN 0-9628301-0-0
Copyright © 1990 by Mark Bishop
P.O. Box 14121
Panama City Beach, Florida 32407
U.S.A.

Published by Mark Bishop Ministries
P.O. Box 14121
Panama City Beach, Florida 32407
U.S.A.

# Dedication

This book is dedicated to the late Donald P. Stephenson, my beloved father-in-law, who was used of God to take a boy and make him into a man; and to my daughters Virginia Lee and Victoria Grace, in whose eyes I can see those same virtues and qualities of their grandfather that so inspired my life. Even so, come Lord Jesus (I Thessalonians 4:13-18).

# Contents

# Acknowledgement

As one looks back upon his or her past, there always stand out certain ones whose faces shine as beacons of love and help. As I reflect upon these many people God has brought my way to deposit so many special blessings, I am in awe. He has blessed me with very special friends, associates and teachers in the Lord. It is in this space that I would like to give a special acknowledgement to them for their ministry to me.

A very special word of gratitude goes to my spiritual teacher and "father in the Lord", Kenneth E. Hagin, whose Holy Ghost filled words and godly example have formed the very guidelines of God's Word by which I live my life. To my wife Scarlett, whose prayers have upheld me during the most crucial years of my life, those spent in the ministry. To Holy Ghost friends Patsy Cameneti, Willie George, Kenneth and Gloria Copeland, and Rudy Vrtachnik who have been a special cheering section and inspiration in my walk with God.

I would also like to mention a special acknowledgment to Guy Duininck, whose appreciation of the message of this book encouraged its writing and motivated its publication, and whose valuable insights and special editing skills enable this important message to be communicated with clarity and precision.

And, of course, all the praise and honor to my Lord Jesus, without Whom I am nothing and without Whom this message would not be possible. For it was by the divine visitation of a dream and by a revelation of God's Word that my eyes were opened to see this powerful truth of Spiritual Jurisdiction.

Psalms 110:3 so beautifully describes my life and the ministry that God has entrusted into my care, for "it is He that hath made me, and not me myself..."

Mark Bishop
November, 1990

# Preface

In 1985 our church was in the first phase of its building program. This was a very hectic and demanding time for me as the pastor because we had decided to do the majority of the construction ourselves. Along with the regular aspects of pastoring, such as counseling and teaching the Word, hours of building related administration and supervision filled each day.

Because of these extra demands, God specially prepared me to minister the Word. Very often He would speak within my own spirit the full message for each service, in complete outline form, right down to every scripture, within a matter of minutes. Truly this was a special endowment of His grace to help me and our congregation through that demanding time.

On two occasions, however, God supernaturally imparted His message to my heart while I was asleep. One of these messages came in an outline form; like a prepared sermon. The other came like a movie picture, after which God woke me up and expounded upon what I had seen and heard in my dream.

This dream, that occurred in June of 1985, God called *"Spiritual Jurisdiction."* Through this dream He revealed to me truths and laws of the spirit realm that govern both the extents and the limitations of all spiritual authorities. It became very plain to me why Satan was able to attack believers' lives. It became clear to me why believers have difficulty walking in complete victory over sin and the devil. It also became very clear to me why God's blessings are sometimes hindered in the lives of Christians.

This message that God supernaturally delivered to me, and that He called "Spiritual Jurisdiction", is one of great importance to the Body of Christ. I have meditated upon the truths concerning Spiritual Jurisdiction and shared them over the past few years. I now feel compelled to condense them to writing and minister them to the whole Body of Christ. This message will instruct and enlighten both young and old in the Lord and will address questions and issues important both to ministers and laymen.

The value of this book rests upon its foundation in the Word of God. Because it is a Biblical and timely message it will be like all scriptural messages; "...profitable for doctrine, for reproof, for correction, for instruction in righteousness: That the man of God may be perfect (or mature), thoroughly furnished unto all good works" [II Timothy 3:16,17] [parenthesis mine]. Those who read and heed what the Holy Spirit has revealed to my heart will experience a new-found power with God and an increase in their authority over the powers of darkness. I say without any hesitation that adherence to the principles in this book will bring a greater anointing on any believer regardless of his or her level of maturity in the Lord. Those who run their race in life acting upon the truths presented in these pages will certainly have a greater peace, a stronger authority, and a more powerful ministry than those who fail to do so!

May this work bless you as it has without fail enriched the lives of all who have listened. And may you grow in grace and power as you study with me about "Spiritual Jurisdiction!"

# Introduction

## Pivotal Principles

As you study God's Word, you will find that there are at least two types of Biblical truths crucial to Christian maturity. The most basic and essential type of truths I refer to as Foundational Truths. Foundational Truths are those truths upon which we build our lives. They are the "first principles of the oracles of God" [Hebrews 5:12]. They are the most basic and most important revelations of God's Word and are necessary for a life of stability in the Lord. Foundational Truths like "The New Birth", "The Baptism in the Holy Spirit", "The Hope of Heaven", and "Faith Toward God" are the building blocks upon which the Christian life must be built.

Another type of truth necessary for Christian maturity I refer to as **Pivotal Principles**. Though not foundational in their nature, they are equally important in helping believers come to full age in the Lord. These Pivotal Principles are spiritual laws upon which other spiritual truths hinge. Jesus' comment after teaching the parable of the Sower and the Seed in Mark 4:13 will serve to clarify what I am saying:

> **"...Know ye not this parable? and how then will ye know all parables?"**

Jesus taught here that understanding other parables hinged upon understanding the parable of the Sower and the Seed. A Pivotal Principle is not the same as a Foundational Truth, but it is very important, for upon these Pivotal Principles hangs greater understanding of Foundational Truths.

If, for example, you do not understand that man is spirit, soul, and body, it will be difficult for you to comprehend the foundational truths of the New Birth and the Baptism in the Holy Spirit. Or if you do not understand the spiritual law of Identification, you will not be able to truly comprehend the foundation of your death, burial, resurrection and ascension with Christ.

Spiritual Jurisdiction is a Pivotal Principle. And upon this spiritual law so many other spiritual truths depend. Failure to gain a working revelation of this basic precept will hinder you from obtaining greater understanding in many other spiritual matters.

In writing this book I have purposed to emphasize the practical applications of the truths I am teaching, focusing on the vital side [the every day use] of the teaching rather than the legal side [pure doctrine]. Rather than going into great depth and detail in expounding upon the legalities of the principles of authority I have purposed to answer questions about why things do not seem to work for us as we were taught they should and then explain how to get them to work.

I felt very much led of the Holy Ghost to present this message in a particular fashion. In the first section I will teach what Spiritual Jurisdiction is. In the following two sections I will expound upon the various practical applications of Spiritual Jurisdiction. After you have grasped the basic principle of Spiritual Jurisdiction you can "feed" on the section that you need the most.

If you desire to be used in a greater way in your ministry you should especially note the section called "Spiritual Jurisdiction and The Ministry." In that section I instruct and encourage, as well as warn, concerning the importance of walking within the boundaries of this law called Spiritual Jurisdiction. Every minister I have shared these truths with has responded with a very hearty, "Amen!"

# Section One

# Defining Spiritual Jurisdiction

## Chapter One

# Don't Be Ignorant of the Things of the Spirit

*"Now concerning spiritual gifts, brethren, I would not have you ignorant."*

**I Corinthians 12:1**

For too long the Body of Christ has been unaware of the operation of the spirit realm. But, thanks be to God, we are waking up. A look at I Corinthians 12:1 will shed light on what God expects of us concerning our knowledge of spiritual operations.

When you read I Corinthians 12:1 from the King James translation you will see that the word *"gifts"* is italicized, denoting that it is not in the original Greek text. The word "gifts" was added at the liberty of the King James translators, hoping to add clarity to the text. But when men tamper with the things of God they often "muddy the water" and mess things up.

The Greek word translated to the English "spiritual gifts" in I Corinthians 12:1 is not the word "charismata", which in I Corinthians 12:4 is properly translated "gifts", but is the Greek word "pneumatikos." It comes from the root word "pneuma", which means "spirit." "Pneumatikos" would be more accurately translated, "the things of the spirit", or simply, "spirituals."

In the study notes of his Annotated Reference Bible, Finis J. Dake states that "pneumatikos" includes all things, both divine and demonic, that operate in and are a part of that realm called the spirit world. To not be ignorant of "pneu-matikos" [things pertaining to the spirit] means much more than just being familiar with the nine gifts of the Holy Ghost. It means to be knowledgeable of and skillful in all things that pertain to the realm of the spirit.

In light of this understanding, a more accurate transla-tion of I Corinthians 12:1 would be, "Now concerning the things of the spirit, brethren, I would not have you ignorant." This more literal translation of this verse causes it to come alive with revelation knowledge!

Paul's exhortation to not be ignorant of the things of the spirit is a preface to the rest of I Corinthians 12 where he teaches about varieties and diversities of ministries. He teach-es about the gifts of the Spirit, the functioning of the body of Christ, and about offices in the church. Paul's introduction in verse 1 is much more than an commandment to not be igno-rant of the gifts of the Spirit. He is saying this: Don't be igno-rant of any operation of the spirit realm.

We need to be knowledgeable of the structure and oper-ation of the <u>entire</u> realm of the spirit. We need to know about God and His ways. We need to understand the operation and ministry of His angels. We need to know about the laws that govern ministry and the anointing for ministry. We must even be aware of and understand the schemes of Satan and the operations of his demonic host.

Some may say, "Now Pastor Mark, we don't need to know anything about the devil!" If that were true, then why did Paul say in II Corinthians 2:11 that we are not ignorant of his devices? Why, then, are we exhorted in Ephesians 6:11-13 to recognize that our battle is not with flesh and blood, but with demonic entities? Why are we encouraged in I Peter 5:8-9 to be aware of Satan's constant enmity against the church? We must be aware of all operations in the spiritual realm including that of Satan and his demons.

It's time for the body of Christ to wake up to the fact that there is a spirit realm. This realm is very real, and in it God, the devil and believers have rights to operate. We need to know about operations in the realm of the spirit if we desire to be co-laborers with God; for "God is a spirit" [John 4:24]. We need to understand the laws and principles that govern the realm of the spirit so that we can flow in that realm like a fish swims in the water!

## Spirituality Vs. Carnality

I was brought up in a church where the definition of carnality was, "one who lives a sinful life." A person who was worldly was considered carnal, while a person who lived a <u>moral life</u> was considered spiritual. Though morality is a very important part of spiritual maturity, a closer look at the Word of God reveals that carnality is not just sin and that spirituality is more than high morals. In Romans 8:5-8 we read,

> **"For they that are after the flesh do mind the things of the flesh; but they that are after the Spirit the things of the Spirit. For to be carnally minded is death; but to be spiritually minded is life and peace. Because the carnal mind is enmity against God: for it is not subject to the law of God, neither indeed can be. So then they that are in the flesh cannot please God."**

Notice that in this scripture the word carnal refers to that person whose mind is fixed upon the natural realm. A carnal person is one who is dominated by the senses; one whose mind is oblivious to the realm of the spirit. To be carnal, then, is to be naturally minded. The person who is spiritual, or spiritually minded, on the other hand, is one who is "after", or who concentrates on and pursues, the things of the spirit. To be spiritual, then, is to be spiritually minded. In the context of this reality we find the true contrast between spirituality and carnality.

As I was studying one day, the Lord opened my eyes to Galatians 5:25. It says,

> **"If we live in the Spirit, let us also walk in the Spirit."**

I had studied many translations of this verse and they all blessed me, but I liked the Holy Ghost's translation best. He said to me, "If we are citizens of the spirit realm, then let's act like it!" That one statement gave me an understanding of what E. W. Kenyon refers to as the legal and vital sides of our walk with God. You see, all believers are legal residents of the spirit realm and members in the family of God. Though we live in this physical world we are strangers and pilgrims to it [I Peter 2:11]. We are only temporary residents of this natural realm. Our real home is with God in heaven. We are citizens of a spiritual kingdom, not just a physical world. We may be in this world, but we are not of it, praise God!

As I meditated further on Galatians 5:25, those strong words of the Holy Spirit continued to explode in my heart, "If we are citizens of the realm of the spirit, then let us act like it!" Let's act like who we are! Let's live our daily lives like the new creations and the supernatural beings we have been created to be!

Being dominated by natural thinking and being oblivious to the realm of the spirit is an aspect of carnality that many overlook. There are many believers who live commendable and holy lives, but because they are so naturally oriented in their thinking, are carnal. If they cannot feel it or see it, then it is not real! Because their thinking is dominated by the natural mind they cannot flow in the Holy Ghost and in the supernatural realm of the spirit. The person whose mind is dominated by the natural realm will have a hard [if not impossible] time flowing with the Holy Ghost and are, by the Bible definition, carnal.

We must realize that being a carnal Christian is more than just being immoral. Carnality also involves ignorance of spiritual matters and the spirit realm. Thank God for morals and holy living. We need to have more of that in the church today. We must not, however, be carnal Christians by being ignorant and unskilled concerning the realm of the spirit.

In I Corinthians 3:1-3, Paul, addressing the carnality at Corinth, rebuked them for, "...walk(ing) as men." The Amplified Bible bears something out from this passage that is interesting to note. It says, "...behaving yourselves after a human standard and like mere (unchanged) men?" (AMP). Acting only in natural ways and living only from the mental realm is to live just like the unsaved. We must replace carnality with spirituality by not being ignorant of the spirit realm.

## Looking to the Unseen

I like what the Apostle Paul wrote by the inspiration of the Holy Spirit in II Corinthians 4:18. He said,

**"While we look not at the things which are seen (the natural, physical realm), but at the things which are not seen (the realm of the spirit!)..." [parentheses mine]**

We need to have our eyes focussed upon and our ears tuned in to the realm of the spirit. We need to see in the realm of the spirit. We need to hear in that realm. We need to walk, talk, pray, sing, and live in that mighty, eternal, all-things-are-possible realm. It is in that realm that God has given birth to us. It is in that realm that we have been delivered out of sin and death and given life by Jesus Christ. It is in that realm that we are raised up together with Him and made to sit in the heavenlies.

If we are citizens and legal residents of the spirit realm, then let's act like it! Let's walk like it! Let's move and live and operate in that realm to which we belong! Let's not pass our lives here on this planet only mindful of our physical surroundings as do the beasts of the field. No, let's soar to the heights of our potential in God and, through the power of the Holy Ghost, be the supernatural, spirit-realm creatures God has called us and created us to be! Concerning the realm of the spirit, brethren (and sisters too), let's not be ignorant, but let us be well-versed, very sensitive, and extremely skilled.

As we study Spiritual Jurisdiction you will become "unignorant" of the spiritual realm by learning about a very important principle that governs its operation. As you grasp this law of the spirit realm called spiritual jurisdiction you will be enabled to function at a higher level of effectualness both in your personal Christian walk and in the ministry to which the Lord has called you.

## Chapter Two

# It Came in a Dream

"And it shall come to pass in the last days, saith God, I will pour out of my Spirit upon all flesh: and your sons and your daughters shall prophesy, and your young men shall see visions, and your old men shall dream dreams:"

**Acts 2:17**

### Hearing from Heaven

A very important key to the supernatural activity of the church is hearing from Heaven. Jesus said in Matthew 16:17-18 that He would build His church on the rock of revelation knowledge. What is revelation knowledge? It is supernaturally imparted information **from** Heaven **by** the Holy Ghost **to** the church. It is upon this foundation of divine revelation from heaven that Jesus said He would build His great army called the church. He will do it by supernaturally imparting information by the Holy Ghost and the devil won't be able to do anything about it.

There is something the Lord showed me from Matthew 16:17-18 that will be a revelation and a challenge to you. In this passage Jesus said,

"...Blessed art thou, Simon Barjona: for flesh and blood hath not revealed it unto thee, but my Father which is in heaven. And I say also unto thee, That thou art Peter, and upon this rock I will build my church; and the gates of hell shall not prevail against it."

9

As I was meditating on this verse of scripture the Holy Spirit said to me, "You have what you have, you are what you are, and you are walking with God where you are walking with God in proportion to how much you have heard from Heaven." Did you get that? The amount of God's plans that you have received from Heaven determines how much of God's will is built into your life. The degree of the blessings of God that you walk in is dependent upon how much you have heard from Heaven and to what degree you walk in the light of what you have heard! The more revelation you receive from God, the further you will progress in God's plan. That much and no more! If you get this truth down in your heart, you will get on your face and seek God and His Word for more of His will for your life! Here is a little poem that came out of my heart concerning revelation knowledge:

> *The more that is revealed*
> *The further you will build.*
> *But you have to seek God,*
> *And to His plans you must yield!*

Hearing from Heaven is vital for the church. In Revelation chapters two and three, Jesus addressed seven different situations in seven different churches, but concluded all His directions with the same exhortation. He said, "He that hath an ear, let him hear what the Spirit saith unto the churches" [Revelation 2:7, 11, 17, 29; 3:6, 13, 22]. No matter what you are faced with, your response remains the same. You must seek the Lord and hear what the Spirit has to say. Hearing from Heaven will cause you to gain the great victories promised for your life.

Thank God for mental knowledge of His Word. Thank God for the renewing of our minds. But hearing from Heaven concerning the application of what we know separates successful living from mere knowledge. That's what James meant when he wrote, "If any of you lack wisdom, let him ask of God..." [James 1:5]. If you don't know how to apply the Word of God and the promises of God, seek the Lord for counsel and He will lead you!  Hearing from Heaven gave Joshua the city of Jericho.  Hearing from Heaven gave Jehoshaphat a mighty victory over his foes.  And hearing from Heaven gave the apostle Paul direction for his life and ministry.

## Dreams, One Way God Leads

Supernatural revelation and communication between heaven and earth are to be characteristic of the church age.  God said through the prophet Joel that one of the manifestations of this dispensation would be dreams and visions.  To some, like Brother Kenneth E. Hagin, God speaks in visions.  But God has often spoken to me concerning spiritual things in dreams.

Dreams are one way God can reveal things to the heart of man.  We read in Acts 2:17 that dreams and visions will be part of the church age:

**"And it shall come to pass in the last days, saith God, I will pour out my Spirit upon all flesh: and your sons and your daughters shall prophesy, and your young men shall see visions, and your old men shall dream dreams."**

From the book of Psalms we learn that God can minister to us in the night seasons:

**"I will bless the Lord, who hath given me counsel: my reins (spirit) also instruct me in the night seasons." [parenthesis mine]**

**Psalms 16:7**

Job said this concerning a thought which came to him in the night,

**"Now a thing was secretly brought to me, and mine ear received a little thereof.  In thoughts from the visions of the night, when deep sleep falleth on men,"**

**Job 4:12-13**

There are many other scriptural precedents for being led through the avenue of dreams.  Here are just a few of them:

"But while he thought on these things, behold, the angel of the Lord appeared unto him (Joseph) in a dream..."

Matthew 1:20

"And being warned of God in a dream..."

Matthew 2:12

"And a vision appeared to Paul in the night..."

Acts 16:9

## Dream Saves Church $200,000.00

When our church was first getting established in Panama City Beach, Florida, we were in a little storefront building that was somewhat less than attractive. Our poor location had no parking and was next to a flea market that gloried in its front yard display of used toilets. It was an atrocious sight! In spite of our physical appearance, however, we grew because people were hungry for God's Word.

As we grew, we ran out of room and began to investigate the possibilities of building a new facility. But, as many new churches discover, though we were growing too large for our present facility, we were too small to afford the construction of a new one. All the contractors we counseled with submitted estimated costs twice as high as what we had faith to believe God for!

One night, however, after a beautiful move of the Spirit in a special service, God visited me in a dream. He gave me in detail the design, the floor plan, and the front elevation of the building we were to build. In fact, I actually saw the construction of the building from beginning to end. It occurred over and over again in my dream, like rapid fire machine gun bullets from start to finish, until it was totally burned into my consciousness. When I awoke I was able to draw it on paper and take it to a builder. Not only was the architect very impressed, but we were able to cut the cost of construction almost in half, saving our church over $200,000.00.

Today we enjoy worshipping in the first phase of our overall building program. Our Family Life Center is five times the space of our old facility and seats six times the people. Praise God for Holy Ghost dreams! Thank the Lord for supernaturally imparted information from Heaven.

## How to Judge Dreams

Before I relate the dream God gave me which revealed the principles of spiritual jurisdiction, let me share with you some scriptural guidelines concerning dreams. As with any spiritual experience [whether it be the gifts of the Spirit or visions] dreams must first line up with the Word of God and be submitted to certain scriptural guidelines.

As I have pastored over the years many have come to me and said, "I had a dream last night, what does it mean?" If you don't know what a dream means, then most likely it doesn't mean anything. God deals with us in the <u>revelation</u> of truths, not in the <u>concealing</u> of truths. He doesn't deal with us in riddles. In Acts chapter 10 Peter had a vision that was responsible for the preaching of the Gospel to the house of Cornelius and eventually to the entire Gentile world. God did not just give Peter the supernatural visitation, but also explained what the vision meant and gave him specific instructions on what to do with what he had seen [see Acts 10: 19, 20 and 28].

You see, when God gives you something, you will know what it is about. If you don't know what a dream means, and if you don't have scripture to back it up, then most likely it is not from God. Maybe you had too much pizza the night before or something. If you have to ask what a dream means, it usually doesn't mean anything at all.

I have found that when a person truly receives supernaturally imparted information from the Holy Ghost by way of a dream, some combination of these three things will almost always be present. First, when one awakens he will know supernaturally what the interpretation and/or the application of the dream is. Second, he will have at least two or three scriptures to confirm what has been revealed. Third, there will be an anointing present when he awakens. There will be a keen awareness of the presence of the Holy Spirit. These are some guidelines for judging if a dream is of God or not. All three of these things were present when the Lord taught me by a dream the important and powerful truth called "Spiritual Jurisdiction."

Dreams have been and will continue to be a part of the way God supernaturally imparts information and revelation to His church in this church age. It was by a dream, a Holy Ghost visitation in the night, that God gave me this message of Spiritual Jurisdiction.

## The Dream of Spiritual Jurisdiction

After retiring one evening in June of 1985 I began to have what I would later recognize to be a God-given dream. In this dream, I was standing on a hill with some other people, but was endeavoring to get to another place. I was at point A, but was trying to get to point B. I didn't know exactly where point A was, but I knew that point B represented the will of God.

In my attempt to get from point A to point B [into the will of God] I had to pass through several different territories that seemed to be like counties. Each of these territories had an officer. The officers were demonic-type beings that had jurisdiction in their respective territories. Each time I crossed into another territory the officer that had jurisdiction in that territory would try to capture me. I would run as fast as possible to get to the boundary line where that officers' jurisdiction ended. As soon as I crossed the boundary that defined that demonic officers' jurisdiction it would lay down and whimper or hang its head in defeat.

Upon entering the next territory I would immediately encounter the "demon-officer" who had jurisdiction in that territory and I would begin to run again. One pursuit would end only for another to begin. This pattern of passing through territories and outrunning the "demon-policemen" with jurisdiction in each territory went on and on until I finally passed through the last territory and into the territory which represented the perfect will of God. When I arrived there, I met Jesus. He stood waiting for me holding all the blessings reserved for my life.

When the dream was over, I was immediately awakened by the Holy Spirit. He spoke the words "Spiritual Jurisdiction" out loud to me, burning them into my heart. In conjunction with the words "Spiritual Jurisdiction," He gave me these three verses of scripture:

> "Let every soul be subject unto the higher powers. For there is no power but of God: the powers that be are ordained of God. Whosoever therefore resisteth the power, resisteth the ordinance of God: and they that resist shall receive to themselves damnation. For rulers are not a terror to good works, but to the evil. Wilt thou then not be afraid of the power? do that which is good, and thou shalt have praise of the same: For he is the minister of God to thee for good. But if thou do that which is evil, be afraid; for he beareth not the sword in vain: for he is the minister of God, a revenger to execute wrath upon him that doeth evil. Wherefore ye must needs be subject, not only for wrath, but also for conscience sake."
>
> Romans 13:1-5

> "Who hath delivered us from the power of darkness, and hath translated us into the kingdom of his dear Son:"
>
> Colossians 1:13

> "Know ye not, that to whom ye yield yourselves servants to obey, his servants ye are to whom ye obey; whether of sin unto death, or of obedience unto righteousness?"
>
> Romans 6:16

As I reflected upon this amazing dream over the next day and meditated on the scriptures the Lord gave me, I began to see a powerful principle which governs all activity in the realm of the spirit. This principle called spiritual jurisdiction operates in conjunction with the law of authority in the realm of the spirit.

In the next few chapters I will share with you some tremendous truths I have learned in relationship to this dynamic principle of spiritual jurisdiction. I will answer questions about why we do not walk in the blessings of God even though they have been promised to us. I will answer questions about why the devil is able to successfully attack believers and will teach you how to walk out of his range at all times. I will teach you about your own spiritual jurisdiction and range of authority. In addition to this, we will discuss boundaries of authority in ministry. Boundaries and borders which, if not recognized, respected, and obeyed, will short-circuit the anointing in individual's ministries and possibly shorten their lives.

Learning about spiritual jurisdiction will bring you to a greater depth of understanding concerning all aspects of your Christian life. It will serve to open your eyes to many of the operations in the unseen realm. Every aspect of your life — your relationship with God, your ongoing warfare with Satan and demonic principalities, and even the success of your ministry — hinges on this spiritual reality. Follow me through God's Word as we unveil the secrets of Spiritual Jurisdiction.

## Chapter Three

# Understanding Spiritual Jurisdiction

**"Let every soul be subject unto the higher powers. For there is no power but of God: the powers that be are ordained of God. Whosoever therefore resisteth the power, resisteth the ordinance of God: and they that resist shall receive to themselves damnation. For rulers are not a terror to good works, but to the evil. Wilt thou then not be afraid of the power? do that which is good, and thou shalt have the praise of the same: For he is the minister of God to thee for good. But if thou do that which is evil, be afraid; for he beareth not the sword in vain: for he is the minister of God, a revenger to execute wrath upon him that doeth evil. Wherefore ye must needs be subject, not only for wrath, but also for conscience sake."**

**Romans 13:1-5**

Just as the natural realm is governed by laws and principles, so also is the realm of the spirit. The natural realm is governed, for example, by the law of gravity, the laws of electricity, and the laws of aerodynamics. These laws control functions in the natural, physical realm. In the same way there are laws which govern operations in the realm of the spirit.

Romans 3:27 declares that there is a law of faith. This law of faith governs the use of power in the spirit world. Love is called the "royal law" in James 2:8. In Romans 8:2 we are introduced to the "law of the Spirit of Life in Christ Jesus" which supersedes the law of sin and death. These are just a few of the laws which govern the realm of the spirit. Just as failure to recognize and adhere to the natural laws God has designed will always prove to be physically disastrous, so failure to recognize and adhere to the spiritual laws which God has ordained will also prove to be spiritually disastrous.

Let's look briefly at an important spiritual law which governs the operation of all beings in the realm of the spirit and is necessary for grasping the principle of spiritual jurisdiction. This law is called the law of authority.

## The Law of Authority

As you will recall, one of the scriptures the Lord spoke to me when I woke up from my dream was Romans 13:1-5. In verses one and two the word "power" is used several times. This English word "power" is translated from the Greek word "exousia." The word "exousia", however, should be translated "authority." Although authority and power work together, like a hand and glove, they must be recognized as distinct in the realm of spiritual things. Let's replace the word "power" with "authority" and take a more accurate look at Romans 13:1-2:

> "Let every soul be subject unto the higher (authorities). For there is no (authority) but of God: the (authorities) that be are ordained of God. Whosoever therefore resisteth the (authority), resisteth the ordinance of God: and they that resist shall receive to themselves damnation." [parentheses mine]

Romans 13:1-2 teaches about a crucial law which not only governs operations in the natural realm, but also governs operations in the realm of the spirit. This law is the law of authority. The point the Lord made to me from this scripture was this: There is a spiritual law that is ordained by God called the law of authority. This law controls the operation of every spirit-being, and must be recognized and adhered to.

The law of authority was ordained by God. He instituted it and every spiritual being, including ourselves, must cooperate with it. In fact, the Lord spoke to my heart after the dream and said that this law of authority is one of the greatest keys to understanding and operating in the realm of the spirit. He also said that those who have trouble submitting to the law of authority will have a very difficult time being used of God. In recognizing the law of authority we can begin to understand the significance of the principle of spiritual jurisdiction.

## What is Spiritual Jurisdiction?

Jurisdiction can be defined as "a range of authority." Range means "scope, boundaries, limitations, or distance." Authority means "the right to command, enforce, or intervene in a matter." Jurisdiction, then, means the right to exercise authority within a specific region or territory. A specific jurisdiction is the range, scope, boundaries or region in which one has the right to command, enforce or intervene in a matter. Now let's expand our definition of jurisdiction to include the realm of the spirit.

A spiritual jurisdiction is, "the boundaries within which a spirit being has the right to command, enforce, intervene or exercise power in the realm of the spirit." All spirit beings have a range or region within which they do have the right to exercise and enforce power. Conversely, all spirit beings have boundaries outside which they do not have the right to exercise or enforce power. This is the law of spiritual jurisdiction.

God has a spiritual jurisdiction. Angels have a certain spiritual jurisdiction. Men, both saved and unsaved, have a spiritual jurisdiction. Satan and his demonic cohorts have a certain spiritual jurisdiction. The boundary lines of a specific spiritual jurisdiction may be geographic, as with cities, states, or even nations, but mainly these boundaries pertain to established laws in spiritual matters and spiritual offices. Spiritual Jurisdiction is the law of authority which governs the operation of all beings in the realm of the spirit.

Recognizing the principle of spiritual jurisdiction is vital in all things pertaining to the believer's life. It has implications concerning our relationship with God, our warfare with the enemy, our authority as believers, and our various calls to ministry. In order to understand your place in spiritual matters and operate in your authority you must understand this principle of spiritual jurisdiction.

Having established the basic definition of Spiritual Jurisdiction, let's focus on how this principle really works.

## Three Authorities in One World

We must understand that there are three spiritual authorities that have rights to operate. These three authorities are God, Satan, and man. Some picture the spirit realm as a crazy, haphazard, unorganized world where it is impossible to predict what is going to happen. That, however, is not true. You see, no kingdom, no system, and no realm can function without levels of authority. There is a law of authority, of rank and order, in the spirit realm. Every being in the spirit realm must operate within the restraints of its boundaries of authority. The realm of the spirit is a highly organized and structured world and is governed by the law of spiritual jurisdiction.

There are boundaries and borders that measure out the extent and limitations of authority of every being in the realm of the spirit. Just as the natural realm has boundaries defining the range of police jurisdiction, so there are boundaries in the spirit realm that outline the range of authority of Satan, of demons and angels, of the believer, of ministerial offices and anointings, and even boundaries God has outlined for Himself that He will not transgress!

In the God-head there is rank and authority. Jesus is submitted to the Father, and the Holy Spirit is submitted to the Father and the Son [I Corinthians 11:3].

God's angels have rank and order. Daniel chapter 10 speaks of chief angels and the higher angels. Michael and Gabriel are examples of such higher angels. In God's kingdom there are cherubim and seraphim and a variety of different angels with different duties and assignments, and different levels of authority. None of them step outside their level of authority or their rank.

Satan's kingdom is also governed by a highly organized and structured system of rank and order [see Ephesians 6:11-13]. The law of authority governs the activities of his demonic forces.

If you are a student of the Bible you will have already learned that there is rank and order in the Body of Christ. Bless God, we need to act like the army that God is calling us to be. We need to endure hardness, follow orders, submit to those over us in the Lord, and quit breaking rank!

In my dream of Spiritual Jurisdiction, these three authorities were present; God, Satan [represented by the demon policemen] and man [represented by me]. I recognized that there were extents and limitations to God's authority, to Satan's authority, and to the authority which I had as a believer. There was a jurisdiction within which God **was** able to bless me and outside of which He **was not**. There was a jurisdiction within which the demons had authority to harass me and outside of which they could not. I also had a jurisdiction which was represented by my right to choose which authority I would submit to. There were limitations and boundaries concerning all three of these authorities.

Failure to recognize that God, Satan, and man all have established boundaries within which they have a right to operate and outside of which they do not will keep us from understanding why things happen as they do. We will not know why certain things happen to believers. We will not know who is exercising authority and, therefore, will not know who to resist or when to resist. We will not be able to recognize if God is doing something or if it is the devil. We will not understand when to take spiritual initiative and when to rest in faith. We will not recognize that there are limitations even to God's ability to bless us. We will not understand why our legal authority in Christ seems, at times, to be short-circuited and why Satan seems to be free to exercise his power.

We must recognize the extent and limitations of the boundaries of God's authority. We need to know that outside certain boundaries He cannot bless us. But we must also realize that within certain boundaries He can and will.

We must realize that Satan has certain boundaries within which he can exercise authority. Within certain boundaries he has authority to harass and torment. But, as I learned from the dream and as we will discover from God's Word, we can step out and stay outside of Satan's boundaries where he and his demons must desist their maneuvers in our lives.

We must also realize that there are boundary lines outside of which we, as believers, cannot exercise our authority. Within specified boundaries, however, we can exercise our rights and reign as kings in this life. Recognizing and operating within these laws of authority is one of the greatest keys to operating effectively in the realm of the spirit.

There are levels of authority in the realm of the spirit. Every being must operate within the boundaries of their authority. When we understand the law of authority and recognize the important place it has in the realm of the spirit, we will begin to understand the important principle of spiritual jurisdiction.

In the next section we will explain the jurisdiction of Satan, the jurisdiction of God, and the jurisdiction of the believer. In so doing we will gain great insight and will be filled with spiritual understanding that will greatly increase the effectualness of our Christian walk. In Section III we will explore boundaries that apply to ministry in the body of Christ. Understanding ministerial jurisdiction will keep you in your right place in the body of Christ and will also make you as effectual as possible.

# Section Two

# Applying
# Spiritual
# Jurisdiction

## Chapter Four

# Satan's Jurisdiction

**"But if our gospel be hid, it is hid to them that are lost: In whom the <u>god of this world</u> hath blinded the minds of them that believe not..."**

**II Corinthians 4:3,4**

People are often unaware that Satan has authority in this world. There is, however, a domain within which he has the right to exercise his power. This domain is known as Satan's kingdom and in his kingdom he has the right to enforce his power. Another way of expressing this truth is simply to say that Satan has a spiritual jurisdiction. He has a realm within which he has the right to enforce his will.

It is crucial that believers recognize and define Satan's jurisdiction. In this way they can avoid the deceptive devices he uses against them. Knowing the boundaries of Satan's authority will keep believers from falling into the pitfalls and traps that he spreads before the feet of God's people.

## Defining Satan's Kingdom

When Adam yielded himself to sin in the garden of Eden, he transferred to Satan the jurisdiction which God had entrusted to man. Through Adam's fall Satan gained the right to operate upon this earth and gained legal authority over people. He established a kingdom and an operating system and took a place of spiritual jurisdiction in this world. He is the ruler of the kingdoms of this world, the ruler over demonic entities, and the ruler over those who have not been translated out from under his authority through the work of Christ.

Jesus confirmed this reality on several occasions. In John 12:31 and in John 16:11 Jesus called Satan the "prince [or ruler] of this world." And in Matthew 12:26 Jesus clearly revealed that Satan has a kingdom by saying,

> **"...if Satan cast out Satan, he is divided against himself; how then shall his kingdom stand?"**

Satan himself claimed jurisdiction and revealed how he came to possess it. In Luke 4:6 he told Jesus that the kingdoms of this world had been delivered to him and that, "...to whomsoever I will I give it."

The devil's kingdom is not the planet called earth, but rather the world, or this world system. The earth is the Lord's and the fullness thereof. But this world system, dominated by the powers of greed and lust, is Satan's domain. In II Corinthians 4:4 he is called, "...the god of this world..." This scripture is clear and strong. By calling Satan, "god", the Bible definitely signifies that he has authority. And by calling him the god of "this world" the Word of God clarifies that there is a particular realm in which he has authority.

We must define the extents and limitations of his right to operate. We must define what he has a legal right to do and what he does not have a legal right to do. We must clearly define his kingdom and mark the borders of his legal jurisdiction. How can we identify Satan's kingdom? How can we locate the boundaries of his jurisdiction?

Satan's kingdom cannot be defined by geographical boundaries or by any naturally visible borders. It can, however, be defined these two ways: First, by identifying those over whom he can legally exercise authority. Second, by defining the forces that govern the world system in which he is lord.

First, let's consider the boundaries of Satan's jurisdiction by asking the question, "Over whom can Satan exercise authority?" In the answer to this question we will see that Satan has different rights relative to demons, unbelievers, and believers.

Concerning demonic forces Satan has unlimited authority because they chose to obey him in the heavenly insurrection. Satan's right to use his authority extends over all the demons which fell with him from heaven. He is called the prince of the authority of the air [Ephesians 2:2]. The word "air" signifies that sphere in which the demonic forces operate [Vine's]. He is, then, the "archon" [greek], or ruler, of that sphere in which demonic forces operate. The New English Bible calls him, "the commander of the spiritual powers of the air..." Satan is chief of and has full authority over all demonic entities. The whole demonic kingdom falls under his jurisdiction.

Satan also has jurisdiction over some people. He has authority through the law of sin and death over all unsaved people. In Ephesians 2:2 he is called, "...the spirit that now worketh in the children of disobedience." Those who are in rebellion to God, those not born again, are under Satan's jurisdiction and rulership. Ephesians 6:12 says that Satan is the, "ruler of the darkness of this world." Within this world system with it's lust and darkness Satan is "god." He has authority and, therefore, power over the citizens that choose to inhabit the spiritual territory called "this world."

Satan's rights in respect to the unbeliever are almost limitless. He is the unbeliever's god and father and they are all legal subjects of his kingdom. He has the right to blind them and totally bind them up in his chains and fetters of sin and death.

Concerning the believer, however, Satan only has certain **limited** rights. These rights differ from his rights with unbelievers and with demons. Satan has the right to tempt, test and confront [Ephesians 6:13,16]. Satan has the right to *attempt* physical attack. Satan has the right to *attempt* to plant thoughts in our minds [John 13:2; Acts 5:3]. Satan has the right to roam about throughout the earth and *attempt* to devour [I Peter 5:8]. Satan has the right to *attempt* control and deception [I Timothy 4:1]. He can *attempt* to wield power and influence over us. He has the right to give the kingdoms of this world to whomsoever he will [Luke 4:6]. He has the right to accuse the brethren [Revelation 12:10]. Satan can also *attempt* to bring upon the believer other works of his kingdom. He can attempt to inflict sickness, fear, poverty, depression, lust, hate, greed, and division.

The reason Satan has the right to attempt to inflict the believer in these various ways is because we share this planet with him. Note again, however, that Satan does not have the right to devour, only the right to *attempt* to devour. He can only challenge our authority in Christ. Any further rights Satan may have beyond the right to challenge are determined by the believer.

Satan's jurisdiction can also be defined by his limitations concerning the believer. Satan does not have the right to stay when resisted by the believer [James 4:7]. Satan does not have the right to make the believer sin [Romans 6:13]. He cannot tempt us beyond what we are able to resist [I Corinthians 10:13]. He does not have the right to separate us from the love of God which is in Christ Jesus [Romans 8:38-39]. And Satan cannot steal our salvation [John 10:28-29].

Over these three groups of beings — demons, unsaved individuals, and believers — Satan has certain rights to enforce his power.

Secondly, Satan's kingdom can be recognized by the forces that operate within his sphere of influence. These forces include fear, strife, rebellion, disobedience, pride, and many other lusts. When an individual, saved or unsaved, is walking under the influence of these forces, they are surely walking in the devil's territory; well within his jurisdiction. The practical application of this truth will be elaborated on in chapter six.

The boundaries of Satan's jurisdiction in this world system are also defined by time. In the account of the Gadarene demoniac, the demon in control asked Jesus the question, "...art thou come hither to torment us before the time?" [Matthew 8:29] Satan's duration of operation extends from the time of Adam's transgression until he is bound up during the millennial reign. After this one thousand year period he will be loosed and will have jurisdiction for another short period of time. Finally he will be judged and eternally bound and his jurisdiction will cease forever. Hallelujah! [See Revelation 20:1-10]

Satan's jurisdiction includes his control over demons, his deceptive power to blind the unsaved, and his right to attempt to enforce his power over the believer. Within this world system, over certain classes of persons, and for a specific length of time Satan can rightfully exercise his power. All these extents and limitations mark the borders of Satan's jurisdiction.

## We Have Been Legally Delivered From Satan's Jurisdiction

**"Who hath delivered us from the power (authority)of darkness, and hath translated us into the kingdom of his dear Son:"**

**Colossians 1:13**

As believers we have been delivered from the devil's authority. Colossians 1:13 declares, "Who (God) hath delivered us from the power (*"exousia"* — authority or jurisdiction) of darkness and hath translated us into the kingdom (or jurisdiction) of His dear Son." In this scripture we again find that the Greek word "exousia" has been translated "power." But "exousia" means authority, or jurisdiction. Believers have been delivered out of the jurisdiction of darkness and translated into the jurisdiction of God!

Here in the midst of the reality of our redemption we find the law of spiritual jurisdiction. By the blood of Jesus and through His death, burial, and resurrection we have been translated out of Satan's kingdom into God's. We have been transferred out of the realm where the devil has legal authority and become citizens of God's domain.

The word "translated" in Colossians 1:13 comes from two Greek words which mean "change" and "to stand." We were standing in the kingdom of darkness under Satan's authority, but our place of standing has changed. We have been brought out of his kingdom and have been made to stand strong and secure in God's kingdom!

Remembering that the definition of jurisdiction is, "the range of authority" or "the boundaries within which authority can be exercised" we can see a fresh new picture of what Colossians 1:13 is teaching. We have been delivered out of the realm where Satan has authority into the region where Jesus is Lord! We have been transported out of Satan's range! In fact, you could translate this verse by saying that, "We have been translated out of the devil's jurisdiction into God's jurisdiction!"

## *Seated in Heavenly Places*

I grew up in the southern rural suburbs of Birmingham, Alabama. Although the community in which we lived would not have been considered a farming area, many of the people did own larger than average tracts of land. Our family had 90 acres which provided plenty of room for a boy to enjoy dogs, horses, and even a few cows. It was a wonderful playground for an adventuresome young lad.

The surrounding wooded areas provided a very safe atmosphere for many outdoor activities including a place for us to hunt and to shoot guns. Occasionally we would hunt quail or doves, but most of the time we just "plinked around" at trees or other inanimate targets. Growing up shooting guns, however, my brother Rick and I developed one bad habit. In our play with guns we would shoot at large airline jets that flew over our house.

These jumbo jets and 747's were flying at least 30,000 feet above the ground as they passed over our house. Our small pellet guns or light rifles could at best shoot 2,000 feet straight up. As these jets glided across the beautiful blue skies with such grace and glory, we ever so diligently fired away at them from down below. Our shooting, however, was to no avail. No matter how many shells we shot, not one plane crashed in our fields. Looking back I can see how foolish we were. Though we were faithfully firing at those planes from below, there was no way we could do them any damage because they were out of our range!

This story beautifully illustrates one of the truths the Lord wanted me to understand concerning the law of spiritual jurisdiction. There is a region in which Satan has a legal right to operate and within that region he is effective. But believers can learn how to live and operate out of his range!

Legally we are out of the devil's range. We have been seated in heavenly places in Christ Jesus through God's redemptive plan. Ephesians 1:21 tells us that Jesus is positioned "far above all principality and power ("exousia"; authority or jurisdiction) and might and dominion..." And Ephesians 2:6 says that God has also raised us up together and made us sit together in heavenly places in Christ Jesus. We have been raised up out of Satan's range!

Legally we are just like those silver jumbo jets that flew over my house when I was a boy. The jets were out of the range of our bullets. And legally believers are outside the scope of Satan's authority and out of his jurisdiction! Legally he has no right to exercise power in our lives!

Legally Satan has no more right to enforce power over you than would a Tennessee sheriff in a Texas county. Although the Tennessee sheriff has a badge and a gun [he has power], he doesn't have the authority to use it outside the boundaries of his jurisdiction.

Though we are legally free from Satan's jurisdiction, however, living in the reality of our redemptive position in Christ Jesus is another thing altogether. Living daily in our place of liberty from Satan's authority is where the "rubber meets the road."

This is one of the greatest lessons we can learn from what the Lord taught me concerning the law of spiritual jurisdiction. We can learn how to stay out of Satan's range and how to walk in freedom from his authority.

**Chapter Five**

# Staying Out of Satan's Range

"Who hath delivered us from the power of darkness, and hath translated us into the kingdom of his dear Son:"

**Colossians 1:13**

"Know ye not, that to whom ye yield yourselves servants to obey, his servants ye are to whom ye obey; whether of sin unto death, or of obedience unto righteousness?"

**Romans 6:16**

In the previous chapter we discussed the legal aspect of Satan's jurisdiction in reference to our lives. We learned that we have been delivered out of his jurisdiction and placed into the jurisdiction of Jesus. Contrasting this legal side of our redemption, however, is the vital side. The vital side of our redemption is where we live every day. This is where the "rubber meets the road" so to speak. It is where we manifest in our everyday lives what God's Word declares concerning us. Daily demonstrating Satan's defeat is a desire of all who are redeemed!

Though legally we have a position in the heavenlies outside of Satan's range, it is our responsibility to walk in that position. Though we have been legally redeemed from Satan's rights of lordship and from this world's system, we must "be on our guard" because we are still in this world. Though Satan does not have the legal right to bind us, he does have the right to try. Because we are in this world he has the right to try to exercise authority over us. But though Satan has the right to shoot at us, if we will act upon the Word of God we will stay high above all the power of the enemy. We must learn how to stay out of the devil's range!

We will learn in this chapter that it is one thing to have a place of refuge and safety provided and another thing to dwell there. We will also learn why Satan is able to successfully attack believers and bring defeat into their lives.

## How Satan Defeats Believers

Reflecting back upon my childhood story, I realize that it was to no avail that my brother Rick and I fired away at those high flying jets. They were out of range, thank the Lord! Had one descended, however, below its assigned altitude, it would have been a different matter altogether. If one of those jumbo jets had violated its assigned flight plan and flown over our home at 1,000 feet, we might have been able to shoot the jet down. We might have hit the fuselage in just the right place and blown up the aircraft. Had the pilots been stupid enough to descend within our "range of fire", it could have been disastrous for that aircraft!

This little memoir from my boyhood past illustrates how Satan is able to bring the "planes" of our lives down and "crash" our walk with God. When we "descend" in the spirit by violating Biblical laws, we come within the range of his authority and he becomes successful in our lives. When we get off the assigned flight plan of God's Word we begin to lose altitude. We descend within the range of Satan's fire power and sometimes get hit!

How does a believer fall into Satan's range of assault? How does a believer get into the place where the devil has a right to exercise authority over his life? Let's begin to answer these questions.

## Obeying the Law of Spiritual Jurisdiction

One of the scriptures the Lord gave me when I awoke from my dream was Romans 6:16. In this verse God shared

with me a rule of thumb concerning the law of spiritual jurisdiction. The first part of Romans 6:16 says,

> **"Know ye not, that to whom ye yield yourselves ser-
> vants to obey, his servants you are to whom ye obey..."**

This principle is true of both God's jurisdiction and the
devil's jurisdiction; "...whether of sin unto death or of obedience unto righteousness" [Romans 6:16b]. To whatever
domain you submit yourself, that kingdom will have the
jurisdiction over your life. An understanding of this verse of
scripture helps us realize why Satan can operate his power
in our lives.

Once again we must consider the legal side and the vital
side of our redemption. The legal reality of our redemption
is that Jesus came to destroy the works of the devil [I John
3:8b]. Well, did Jesus do that or not? Certainly He did!
Colossians 2:15 states that Jesus brought Satan to naught.
Why then can Satan still work? Why is he still putting sickness and disease on God's children and producing pain in
their lives if his works have been destroyed?

The answer is simply this. Jesus did not destroy the
works of the devil in the sense that Satan is completely disal-
lowed to operate in the earth any more. Rather, Jesus
destroyed the works of the devil by providing a place in Himself where the believer can be sheltered from Satan's destruction. If we live in the world we will have trials and tribulation, but if we live in Christ, though we be "shot at", we will
still overcome!

When the believer yields to any work of Satan's kingdom he places himself in Satan's jurisdiction and, thus, under
his power. A believer is not under Satan's jurisdiction in
respect to his legal status, but if he yields himself to the works
of Satan's kingdom he will certainly at that time be under
Satan's jurisdiction. Whenever a believer is disobedient to
God he becomes subject to Satan's authority.

Let's look at two scriptures which illustrate this truth. I
John 5:18 states:

**"We know that whosoever is born of God sinneth not; but he that is begotten of God keepeth himself, and that wicked one toucheth him not."**

Notice that the believer, "keepeth himself." It is up to us to fly in the assigned flight plan of God's Word and keep our altitude high enough that Satan cannot touch us. God has provided everything we need to soar in those heavenly heights, but it is our job as "pilots" to keep our lives on course! Though we cannot keep the devil from shooting at us, we can keep our lives out of his effective range!

Another scripture that illustrates our responsibility in staying out of the devil's jurisdiction is Psalms 91. Notice that in verses 1 through 3 and again in verses 9 through 16 God's Word emphasizes our responsibility in keeping ourselves outside the enemy's range,

**"He that dwelleth in the secret place of the most High shall abide under the shadow of the Almighty... Because thou hast made the Lord, which is my refuge, even the most High, thy habitation; There shall no evil befall thee, neither shall any plague come nigh thy dwelling...Because he hath set his love upon me, therefore will I deliver him: I will set him on high, because he hath known my name."**

**Psalms 91: 1,9,10,14**

Notice how divine protection is experienced. It was experienced by the psalmist only as he chose to dwell in the secret place of the Most High. In that place God had total jurisdiction and, therefore, the psalmist remained out of range of the enemy's attacks! Had the psalmist not chosen the secret place of the Almighty for his lodging, or had he not made the Lord his habitation, then he could not have experienced the assurance of this life of safety.

When the believer places himself in the protective jurisdiction of the Lord, he also places himself in the realm which is outside the activity of destruction. The believer is assured of total protection and safety when he has chosen the high altitudes of the presence of God to be his daily flight plan. If you walk in the light of God's Word and in obedience to the laws that govern God's jurisdiction, then you are under the rule of His Lordship. You are out of the devil's range.

The opposite, however, is also true. If you walk in darkness [sin, strife, anger, doubt, etc.] then even though you have been <u>legally</u> freed from Satan's jurisdiction, you have put yourself back within his jurisdiction and within his range of attack. This is what Romans 6:16 declares: **You become a subject in the kingdom to which you yield yourself servant. You become slave to the one to whom you yield your life**. Though we are legal citizens of God's kingdom, the boundary lines that we choose to reside within will, by our choice, define the domain which has jurisdiction in our lives.

## Give No Place to the Devil

Ephesians 4:27 says, "...neither give place to the devil." Evidently we, as believers, can give place or we would not have this warning from God.

We give the devil place in our lives and allow him to successfully attack us when we yield to the activities within his jurisdiction. We actually give the devil place when we choose to travel through or dwell within the domain of darkness that he presides over. Let's look at some of the ways we descend into the devil's territory and give him jurisdiction in our lives.

### *Attitudes*

We can lose altitude in the spirit with wrong attitudes toward the things of God. I like what Dr. John Maxwell said in his book <u>Be All You Can Be</u>. He states, "Your attitude determines the altitude at which you soar in life." We can certainly see this truth in Deuteronomy 28:47,48:

> **"Because thou servedst not the Lord thy God with joyfulness, and with gladness of heart, for the abundance of all things; Therefore shalt thou serve thine enemies which the Lord shall send against thee, in hunger, and in thirst, and in nakedness, and in want of**

**all things: and he shall put a yoke of iron upon thy neck, until he have destroyed thee."**

We can learn from this verse that even though we belong to the Lord, if we don't serve Him with the right attitude of joy we can open up the door to the devil. When we have wrong attitudes we lower our altitudes and descend within Satan's range of power!

The apostle Paul warned the church at Corinth about the attitudes represented by murmuring and complaining. In I Corinthians 10:10 he reminded them that when the children of Israel complained, fiery serpents began to destroy them. This record of Israel's sin was written so that we could learn from Israel's mistakes and not step outside of the blessings of God into the "fiery bites of serpents."

When we allow the wrong attitudes about life to overcome us, we allow ourselves to be lowered into the spiritual jurisdiction of the devil! This is, many times, how the devil is able to "hit" Christians. As elementary as these things may sound, it is amazing that many Christians are either ignorant of, or fail to live by, these very real governing principles of God.

### Works of the Flesh

When we yield to any work of the flesh such as pride, fear, strife, anger, or lust and, thus, get involved in sin through disobedience to the instructions of God's Word and the Holy Spirit, we veer off course and lose altitude. Consider the evil work of strife as an example. When a believer gets into strife, he actually places himself within the jurisdiction of the devil. James 3:14-16 says,

> **"But if ye have bitter envying and strife in your hearts, glory not, and lie not against the truth. This wisdom descendeth not from above, but is earthly, sensual, devilish. For where envying and strife is, there is confusion and every evil work."**

Strife is not "from above", but is "devilish." Where strife is, there is every evil work. Strife pulls you out of your heavenly position in Christ down into the realm of earthly and devilish activity.

James also teaches in James 1:14-15 that lust leads to sin which leads to death, and we know that death is of the devil. Paul told Timothy in II Timothy 2:24-26 that those who entered into strife must, "...recover themselves out of the snare of the devil, who were taken captive by him..."

Descending into Satan's jurisdiction will also result if one yields to demonic spirits. When a person submits to a particular demon's influence, then that spirit gains a level of jurisdiction in their life.

When a believer walks in disobedience to God's Word and His will, they get on the devil's territory and he has a right to attack them. Yielding to works of the flesh or demonic influence, whether strife, lust, or anything else, gives Satan jurisdiction in believers' lives.

Satan cannot launch successful attacks against us unless we yield to fleshly and demonic works like fear, doubt, strife or sin. In fact, when we stand firm trusting God's Word, we can "pass through the fire and not be burned." There are so many beautiful scriptures like Psalms 23:4 and Isaiah 43:1-3 that teach us if we walk in the Lord we can pass through real storms and not even be phased! Right in the presence of our enemies we can have a table of God's provision spread before us!

### *Ignorance of the Word*

Another way that we give place to the devil and get over onto his "turf" is through ignorance of God's Word. When we are ignorant of the Word we are ignorant of God's will, ignorant of Satan's operations, and ignorant of our authority as believers. Hosea 4:6 says that God's people perish for a lack of knowledge. II Corinthians 2:11 says,

> **"Lest Satan should get an advantage of us: for we are not ignorant of his devices."**

Satan cannot get advantage over us when we are aware of his devices. Not being ignorant means that Satan cannot gain an advantage over us. But if we are ignorant it is possible for him to gain the upper hand.

I Peter 5:8 reveals that if believers don't stay sober minded and aware of Satan's activity, then through ignorance he will take advantage of them. Ignorance of operations in the realm of the spirit is not bliss. Sometimes it can cost you your life!

The Word of God is like an earth suit that protects us from the "hostile" and contaminating environment we live in. The Psalmist declared in Psalms 17:4, "...by the word of thy lips I have kept me from the paths of the destroyer." In John 17:14-19, Jesus spoke this same truth concerning the ability of God's Word to protect us from the enemy while we live in his domain,

> **"I have given them thy word; and the world hath hated them, because they are not of the world, even as I am not of the world. I pray not that thou shouldest take them out of the world, but that thou shouldest keep them from the evil (one) ...Sanctify them through thy truth: thy word is truth. As thou hast sent me into the world, even so have I also sent them into the world. And for their sakes I sanctify myself, that they also might be sanctified through the truth."**

In Luke 4:1-13, Jesus was shot at by the devil, but because He stayed within the boundaries of God's Word He was not hit. Though He was tempted by Satan, He responded each time by saying, "It is written." Not only did knowledge of the Word of God protect Him from Satan's authority, but His relationship and fellowship with the Father remained intact. By staying within the boundaries of the written Word of God, Jesus ran Satan off the mountain that day and also received blessings from the Lord in the form of ministry from the angels [Matthew 4:11].

Jesus taught in Luke 6:46-49 that when we act on the Word, living within the boundaries of what God has said, then the storms will not be able to shake our lives.

All our protection from the power of the devil and the work of his cohorts comes from abiding in the Word. I John 1:7 states,

> **"But if we walk in the light, as he is in the light, we have fellowship one with another, and the blood of Jesus Christ his Son cleanseth us from all sin."**

When we walk in the light, that is, when we walk in the revelation of God's Word, then the blood of Jesus operates in our lives not only as the cleansing agent, but also as the protecting agent.

A believer who is ignorant of what belongs to him according to God's Word is a believer who is walking unprotected and unarmed in life's war.

### Failing to Stand

Another way we give place to the devil is simply by failing to take a stand against him. James 4:8 states that as we resist the devil, he will flee. Satan does not have a legal right to devour the believer, but because he is an outlaw, he will "break the law" and function as he wills until someone exercises authority over him. It is not only important to have knowledge of God's Word, but to consciously and aggressively act upon that knowledge. It is not only important to have knowledge of Satan's devices and your authority over him, but you must resist him and refuse him any room to operate in your life.

I Peter 5:8-9 exhorts us to stand steadfast against the enemy,

> **"Be sober, be vigilant; because your adversary the devil, as a roaring lion, walketh about seeking whom he may devour. Whom resist steadfast in the faith..."**

In Ephesians 6:11-14 we find this same truth,

**"Put on the whole armour of God, that you may be
able to stand against the wiles of the devil...and having
done all, to stand. Stand therefore..."**

Many believers fail to recognize the totality of what Jesus
meant in Matthew 16:19 when he said, "...I will give unto thee
the keys of the kingdom of heaven." He went on to state that,
"Whatsoever thou shalt bind on earth shall be bound in heaven:
And whatsoever thou shalt loose on earth shall be loosed in
heaven." Jesus was simply saying that what we allow God
allows. What <u>we</u> **allow** the devil to do, he has the **right** to do
by default and neglect on our part.

Jesus said in John 17 that we are in the world, but are not
of the world. In John 16:33 Jesus said that in the world we
would have tribulation, but I John 5:4 teaches us that the victory that overcomes the world is our faith. Faith, which is an
aggressive stand on God's Word, is a must if we desire to
quench all the fiery darts of the enemy.

### *Fear*

I John 4:18 says that fear has torment. When the believer succumbs to the force of fear he most definitely lowers his
altitude within the range of Satan's jurisdiction. Hebrews
2:14 and 15 teach us that it is through fear that Satan holds
men in bondage,

**"Forasmuch then as the children are partakers of
flesh and blood, he also himself likewise took part of
the same; that through death he might destroy him that
had the power of death, that is, the devil; And deliver
them who through fear of death were all their lifetime
subject to bondage."**

Satan dominates the lives of those who succumb to the
force of fear. God's Word calls this domination bondage. Fear
imprisons one's heart and releases the power of Satan's
destruction in their life. By yielding to fear believers descend
into Satan's range of attack.

42

## *Unforgiveness*

Believers place themselves well within the range of the devil's fiery darts when they choose to walk in unforgiveness and resentment. In Matthew 18:23-35, Jesus taught a parable that explains very clearly and strongly this truth,

> **"And his lord was wroth, and delivered him to the tormentors, till he should pay all that was due unto him. So likewise shall my heavenly Father do also unto you, if ye from your hearts forgive not every one his brother their trespasses."**

**Matthew 18:34,35**

It always troubled me that verses 34 and 35 of this passage seemed to teach that the Lord turns us over to the tormentors if we fail to forgive. It always seemed to contradict the loving nature of our Lord that he would deliver us up to the devil. But when I realized the truth of the law of spiritual jurisdiction, I understood what was really taking place. When we are in blatant and conscious rebellion to a commandment as important as the law of forgiveness, then through that act of disobedience we place ourselves into the enemy's territory of operation.

If I have a guest in my home that has committed a crime, when the police come and ask for him, I have to "deliver him" to the police. So also if we refuse to forgive and choose, therefore, to walk in unforgiveness, when Satan comes to attack us, God is obligated by spiritual law to "deliver" us to the enemy's demands. Thus, Matthew 18:23-35 is not a matter of God punishing us. God doesn't need the help of the devil to teach us lessons. It is a matter of God having to comply with the spiritual laws He has established. Though they were established to protect us, when we break them they result in negative consequences, and even our own harm.

## *Disobedience to the Holy Spirit's Voice*

We can readily see the importance of obeying the written Word of God. But we may fail to respect the personal instructions of God that are spoken to our hearts by the Holy Spirit. Deuteronomy 28:15 says,

> "But it shall come to pass, if thou wilt not hearken unto the voice of the Lord the God, to observe to do all his commandments and his statutes which I command thee this day; that all these curses shall come upon thee, and overtake thee."

Notice here that we are not only instructed to observe all of God's commandments, but we are told to hearken unto His voice. Jesus clearly and specifically said of the Holy Spirit's ministry that He would, "...guide...speak...[and] show us things to come" [John 16:13].

Many times Christians give place to the devil when they fail to heed the directions of the Holy Spirit. One of the clearest examples I know of this reality was the untimely death of my wife's father, Don Stephenson.

For months the Holy Spirit specifically told Don not to turn at a particular intersection which led to the subdivision where he lived. For months he shared with us as a family of the danger that the Lord was communicating to his heart about that particular entrance to his neighborhood. Not only did the Lord warn Don not to turn at that entrance, but instructed him to go down to the next intersection which had a traffic light.

Though he heard this warning for months, Don continued to disobey what the Holy Spirit was saying because it was much quicker and more convenient to turn at the first intersection. But late on Monday night, November 25, 1985, Don was hit and killed by a drunken driver who sped through that intersection without his headlights on.

I know that had Don heeded the voice of the Holy Spirit he would have been protected and spared from that tragedy. Not only would he have been turning at a much more lighted section of highway, which in the natural would have made it possible for him to see the car without its headlights on, but he would have also been within the boundaries of submission to God's protective care through obedience to the voice of the Holy Spirit.

Saints of God, hearkening unto the voice of the Holy Spirit is an essential factor in remaining outside Satan's range of attack. God knows what lies in the future concerning us, and by His Spirit He will help us safely navigate around the snares of the enemy.

## Conclusion

Though Satan may have the right to shoot at us while we live here on this planet, we can walk in the place where his attacks are ineffective against us. Living outside Satan's range of authority by abiding in God, His Word, and in obedience to His Spirit are vital to living the abundant, victorious life that Jesus came to give.

## Chapter Six

# God's Jurisdiction

*"Yea, they turned back and tempted God, and limited the Holy One of Israel."*

**Psalms 78:41**

Is there anything that God can not do? Are there any limitations to His power? Can anyone or anything stop His will from coming to pass? Many would answer these questions with a confident, "NO!" But as you read the Word of God you will find that the answer is actually both yes and no. Though in one sense God is unlimited in His power and can do anything, it is also true that He has placed some limitations upon His operations. For example, Hebrews 6:18 says that it is impossible for God to lie. James 1:13 says that God cannot be tempted with evil. Yes, God is all powerful, but there are limitations He has placed upon Himself that we must understand.

You see, although God is omnipotent and sovereign, He has placed limitations upon Himself in this dispensation; especially in respect to His relationship with man. It is essential that we discern between God's actual power, or His inherent power (i.e. His omnipotence, His omniscience, His omnipresence), and the power He can demonstrate based upon limitations He has established for Himself. In order for us to cooperate with God and receive His blessings we must understand His legal jurisdiction and how He can be limited, especially by our actions. I have divided our study of God's jurisdiction into four areas: God's Jurisdiction and

His will; God's Jurisdiction and His Word; God's Jurisdiction and man's will; and God's Jurisdiction and faith.

## God's Jurisdiction and His Will

In my dream I had to pass through many hostile territories before I entered into the territory that represented the will of God. Each of the territories I ran through represented times in my life when I was not walking in the will of God and, thus, operating in ways that kept me within the jurisdiction of Satan and outside of the blessings of God. As I ran through these hostile territories not only was I harassed by demonic entities, but I was separated from the blessings available to me in the territory I was trying to get to; the territory of the perfect will of God. When I passed through the last jurisdiction of Satan and entered into the jurisdiction of the will of God, Jesus was waiting there holding out blessings for me.

The experience of my dream is very similar to the story of the prodigal son as recorded in Luke 15:11-32. In this story the youngest son forfeited the blessings of his father by leaving father's house and going to foreign lands. In these far away lands he lost his inheritance and became servant to a farmer, eating pig's food. At the point of total despair he was wise enough to return to his father's house knowing that at least his father would take him back as a servant and he would be fed and clothed.

In my dream, because I was a son of God, I was by right an inheritor of blessings. But because I was in the jurisdiction of Satan, I not only forfeited the blessings which were mine, but encountered great difficulties. Because I was outside of "Father's house" I had to pay the consequences of being outside His jurisdiction.

To be in circumstances as I was in my dream, or to be like the prodigal son, does not necessarily require that you be in full rebellion to God. By simply walking in the works of the flesh as stated in Galatians five, you will find yourself outside of the jurisdiction of God [where He has the right to bless you] and inside the jurisdiction of Satan [where he and his cohorts have the legal right to attack you]. The prodigal son forfeited his blessings when he walked out of his father's house. Staying "in the house" — inside the boundaries of the will of God — will keep you in the place where the blessings of God can flow. Leaving "the house" — exiting the boundaries of the will of God — will separate you from the power of God and limit His blessings in your life.

In my dream Jesus was willing to bless me. He was waiting for me, holding forth the blessings as I was attempting to escape from the other territories. He wanted to bless me, but He could not bless me as long as I was submitted to the works of the flesh. As long as I involved myself in activities or attitudes that were outside the will of God, the Lord was unable to give me blessings. Only when I came within the jurisdiction of the will of God could I receive God's blessings. It was only as I drew nigh to Him that He was able to draw nigh to me [James 4:7-8].

In Hebrews 1:9 we see the positive results of staying within the jurisdiction of the will of God. Read here what the Word of God says concerning the Lord Jesus:

**"Thou has loved righteousness (God's jurisdiction), and hated iniquity (Satan's jurisdiction); therefore God, even thy God hath anointed thee with the oil of gladness above thy fellows." [parentheses mine]**

**Hebrews 1:9**

Jesus lived within the boundaries of the perfect will of God, and, therefore, experienced the full measure of the blessings of God. He was not anointed with the oil of gladness just because He was the Son of God. He was anointed with the oil of gladness because He loved righteousness. His measure of blessing was "above His fellows" because He loved righteousness and hated sin. He was blessed because He stayed within the boundaries of the perfect will of God.

God desires to bless us. He has things laid up for us. Ephesians 2:10 states that the Lord has prepared paths ahead of us; paths He has "...before ordained that we should walk in them." But when we wander outside of His will we exit His jurisdiction, thus hindering Him from blessing us.

There is, you see, a good, an acceptable and a perfect will of God [Romans 12:2]. If you are only operating within the "good will" of God then you are probably crossing back and forth between God's jurisdiction and the devil's jurisdiction. When you operate in this manner you will wander in and out of the blessings of God and in and out of the harassment of the devil. That's a dangerous lifestyle for a believer, and yet is the way many believers live.

As I meditated further upon my dream, the Lord pointed out to me that there were **many** territories within which Satan could attack and God could not bless me, but there was only **one** territory within which God could bless me and within which the devil could not successfully attack. That place was within the borders of God's perfect will; within His jurisdiction. When we stay within the boundaries of God's perfect will, He can bless us as He wants to and we will "keep ourselves" from the power of Satan.

In his book "Plans, Purposes, and Pursuits" Brother Kenneth E. Hagin recalls that the Lord spoke to him one time and said, "I bless all of My people <u>as far as I can</u>. But the reason there is not the move of God and the depth of the flow of the Spirit, and the fullness of the manifestation of the Holy Ghost today is because men do not take time to hear from Me. They do not take time to follow My plan set forth in the scriptures. The more closely you follow My plan, the more My power will be in demonstration and in manifestation" [underline mine].

This is one reason that some of us are not receiving the blessings of God. It is not that blessings don't belong to us in Christ. It is not that God does not desire to bless us. It is because we have submitted to works of the flesh rather than to the will of God. It is because we either have not listened for God's plan, or have not carefully followed what we know to be His plan. In so doing we have put ourselves "across the border" from the jurisdiction of God. We have limited God and forfeited His blessings by operating outside His will. Jesus is Lord within His jurisdiction, but He cannot bless us when we "walk" outside His jurisdiction. He cannot bless us to the full extent of His desires if we are outside the boundaries of His perfect will. God's will for your life not only includes the specific instructions of His written word, but also His plan for your life, His call upon your life and His assignments to you in life.

In one of our church services I spoke out these words from the Holy Spirit:

> *"Just as there are many times my children desire to do things for me, but in their resources lack the ability to do what their heart wants to express in deeds.*
>
> *So also does our Heavenly Father shed His tears toward His children below when He cannot reach over and touch them and meet each and every need.*
>
> *But God cannot bless us, no, God cannot supply when our lives are not in union with Him and we are serving the father of lies."*

God wants to bless us all. He wants to meet our needs. But we must live within the boundaries of His power and authority. We must get out of the territory of the works of the flesh. We must get out of the territory of doing our own things our own ways and enter into the territory of God. We must enter into the territory of His perfect will for our lives.

Get out of the devil's jurisdiction and into God's jurisdiction. You will find that the harassment of demonic entities will be broken over your life and you will cross over into the "land of milk and honey"; the territory where the blessings of God always flow!

## God's Jurisdiction and His Word

We must walk within the boundaries of God's will in order to live safely and receive the blessings of His jurisdiction. But what is God's will? Though the specific aspects of God's will for our lives can only be discovered by time in prayer and by following the Holy Ghost, the most basic aspects of God's will are clearly recorded in His Word!

This reality radically changed my life as a young Christian man. For years I had heard from the pulpits of dead denominational churches that it was impossible to know the will of God. Then one day my understanding was opened and I realized that God's will and His Word were one! To abide within the blessed borders of God's jurisdiction and experience His great blessings, one must live within the boundaries of His Word.

God's blessings have always been tied to this condition of walking within the boundary lines of His Word. Believers who expect to experience the <u>blessings</u> of the Christian life without meeting the <u>conditions</u> of the Christian life are ignorant of the Bible and of the operation of spiritual laws. You see, it is not a matter of whether God wants to bless us or not. The fact of the matter is that God cannot bless us if we live outside of obedience to His Word. Over and over again the Lord places the condition of obedience upon the receiving of our needs and the fulfillment of our desires. Deuteronomy 28:1-2 says,

> **"And it shall come to pass, if thou shalt hearken diligently unto the voice of the Lord thy God, to observe and to do all his commandments which I command thee this day, that the Lord thy God will set thee on high above all nations of the earth: And all these blessings shall come on thee, and overtake thee, if thou shalt hearken unto the voice of the Lord thy God."**

Likewise Joshua 1:8 says,

> **"This book of the law shall not depart out of thy mouth; but thou shalt meditate therein day and night, that thou mayest observe to do according to all that is written therein: for then thou shalt make thy way prosperous, and then thou shalt have good success."**

To abide within the scope of God's blessings one must abide within the boundaries of the teachings of His Word.

## God's Jurisdiction and Man's Will

We know that the Lord is sovereign. Yet in His sovereignty He has chosen to limit Himself in His dealings with man. He has limited Himself by giving man a will and, therefore, the freedom to choose whether or not to cooperate with Him and His Word. He has also designed that most of His own operations in the earth would be through the agency of man.

In His dealings with humanity, especially as concerns His desire to bless, God will never violate the human will. Though he desires that all men be saved [I Timothy 2:4 and II Peter 3:9], He will never force anyone to get saved. Though He has the power to rescue and liberate those held captive to sin, and though He has the power to unshackle the prisoners of darkness, He cannot do so until they call upon His name. He cannot rescue those bound by Satan's rule if they choose to continue to live there. Again, God can not because in His omnipotent sovereignty He gave man a will (the right to choose), and has placed that as a limitation over His dealings in our lives.

This reality is clearly demonstrated in the ministry of Jesus. In John 5:1-9 we read the story of Jesus healing a man who had an infirmity for 38 years. Before He could heal this man Jesus had to ask, "Wilt thou be made whole?" Jesus, the Son of God, God in the flesh, had to find out if the man wanted to be healed before He could heal him. He had to know the man's will. The man clarified to Jesus that it was, in fact, his will to be healed by reporting that each time the water of the pool was stirred he tried to get in, but someone always got in before he could. After ascertaining the will of this impotent man Jesus said, "Rise, take up thy bed, and walk."

In Mark 10:46-52 we find the story of blind Bartimeus. After Jesus called Bartimeus to himself he asked him, "What wilt thou that I should do unto thee?" He needed to find out what Bartimeus wanted even though he knew what Bartimeus needed. He needed to know Bartimeus' will concerning his own condition. Bartimeus gave Jesus permission to heal him by telling him that he wanted to receive his sight.

Only then could Jesus say, "Go thy way; thy faith hath made thee whole."

This reality that God will not violate the human will is also seen in the calling of God upon people's lives. He never forces His will on people, but simply invites them to "follow Me." After He makes this invitation, it is up to each person to submit their will to His will. Even Jesus, who ministered as a human being, had to submit His will to the Father in order for the power of God to flow through His life and the plan of God to be accomplished through His death.

## God Has Chosen To Move Through Man

In order for us to understand God's jurisdiction in this physical realm we must recognize the authority which he delegated to man. In the beginning God delegated unto Adam a special authority in this physical world. In so doing, He granted unto mankind a jurisdiction within which he had the right to rule. And though Adam yielded up a part of that authority to the devil in the Garden of Eden, it is still necessary to have a physical body to exercise authority in the earth.

You see, there is a strong relationship between authority in this earth and having a physical body. For God's power and authority to be maximized to its fullest potential in the earth, it must flow through the clay-based vessel of a man; a physical body. This is why Satan desires to possess and control men's lives today. It is so that he can exercise his authority in the earth through the use of their bodies.

As one studies God's Word, he will discover that the omnipotent God of the Universe has chosen to limit Himself to working through the agency of man. In support of this we find certain scriptures such as Ezekiel 22:29-31 which teaches us that in His overall blueprint of the ages, God has chosen to limit His right to deliver men through the prayers of a man,

> **"The people of the land have used oppression, and
> exercised robbery, and have vexed the poor and needy:
> yea, they have oppressed the stranger wrongfully. And
> I sought for a man among them, that should make up**

the hedge, and stand in the gap before me for the land, that I should not destroy it: but I found none."

Romans 5:12-21 is very clear that it was through man that our redemption from sin had to come,

> "...much more the grace of God, and the gift by grace, which is by one man, Jesus Christ, hath abounded unto many...by the obedience of one (man) shall many be made righteous".

**Romans 5:15,19**

This is the mystery of godliness as Paul declared in I Timothy 3:16. God had to become a man in order to exercise His power and authority in the earth and bring redemption to mankind.

From these and other scriptures we understand that God has to have a vehicle, as it were, to move through in this physical world. That vehicle is man. For in this earth realm God has delegated authority to man, and He will not violate nor alter that which He has spoken out of His mouth [Psalms 89:34]. Therefore, God will continue to operate and perform His will in this earth through the vessel of mankind until time as we know it is no more and His plan is complete! This reality is another boundary which defines God's jurisdiction.

## God's Jurisdiction and Faith

A final condition that acts as a border in defining God's limitations and extents to bless is the border of faith. James 1:6-7 and Hebrews 11:6 clearly point this out. James 1: 6-7 says this concerning our receiving the blessings of God:

> "But let him ask in faith, nothing wavering. For he that wavereth is like a wave of the sea, driven with the wind and tossed. For let not that man think that he shall receive anything of the Lord."

God cannot and will not move outside the boundary line of faith. Not only is it impossible to please God without faith, as Hebrews 11:6 declares, but one will also limit God from working in his life without faith.

In Psalms 78:41 we read of how the children of Israel, through doubt, hindered God from blessing their lives,

> **"Yea, they turned back and tempted God and limited the Holy One of Israel."**

God was limited by the lack of faith of the children of Israel. Because they failed to mix faith with God's Word, He could not take them into the promised land of Canaan [Hebrews 4:1-2]. Hebrews 3:19 makes this truth so obviously clear,

> **"So we see that they could not enter in because of unbelief."**

It was not a matter of God's desire to bless Israel that kept them out of the promised land. It was a matter of them not believing what He had clearly spoken. He could not fulfill His declared will and purpose without their cooperation by faith.

Matthew 13:58 says of Jesus that, "...he did not many mighty works there (in Nazareth) because of their unbelief." Mark's gospel says that He, "...could there do no mighty work" [Mark 6:5]. This was not a matter of Jesus' will to heal the sick in Nazareth. It was a matter of His limitations to bless people outside of the boundary line of their faith.

God is the Almighty, all sufficient God of the universe. However, He has placed borders and limitations upon the use of His power and upon the outpouring of His blessings. If the believer ignores this reality it will not only cost him many of the benefits of his covenant with God, but may also lead him to the place where he points an accusing finger at God. If we are not walking in the blessings that God has promised in His Word, it is because we have not positioned our lives in that place where God can use His power to bless and to save. Recognize that there is a range of authority that defines God's power to bless and place yourself within the jurisdiction of His power and love.

## Conclusion

Understanding that God has established borders which define and limit His own exercise of authority in this physical realm helps explain why things happen to believers and why, though we have many promises from God, we seem to experience a low level of blessing in our daily lives. God will not transgress the borders of His jurisdiction. These borders are the borders of His Word, the border of His will, the border of man's will, and the border of faith.

**Chapter Seven**

# The Believer's Jurisdiction

One of the strongest revelations from God's Word ministered in our generation has been the teaching on the Authority of the Believer. Understanding this one truth has helped free many Christians from Satan's manipulations. It is absolutely essential that we understand our legal authority over Satan and his host.

It is just as important, however, that we understand how to exercise that authority. What good is it to us if we know we are free from Satan's power, but don't know how to appropriate our freedom? You see, for every truth of God's Word there is a legal side and a vital side. There is the specific truth, but there is also the practical aspect of walking in that truth.

In this chapter we will take a fresh look at the Authority of the Believer, emphasizing the vital application of this reality and exploring how our authority relates to the principle of spiritual jurisdiction.

## Our Legal Position of Authority

In Ephesians chapters one and two we learn about the legal authority of the believer. Ephesians 1:19-21 reveals that God has positioned His Son in a place of preeminence and power,

> "...according to the working of his mighty power,
> Which he wrought in Christ, when he raised him from
> the dead, and set him at his own right hand in the

> heavenly places, Far above all principality, and power, and might, and dominion, and every name that is named, not only in this world, but also in that which is to come:"

Here we learn that Jesus is positioned in the highest place of spiritual authority. He is seated over all the powers of the enemy.

As we proceed to Ephesians chapter two we discover a marvelous truth concerning our own spiritual position. Not only has God raised Jesus from the dead and positioned Him in a place of authority, but He has also raised us up from the dead and positioned us with Christ in that same place of authority,

> "But God, who is rich in mercy, for his great love wherewith he loved us, Even when we were dead in sins, hath quickened us together with Christ, (by grace ye are saved;) And hath raised us up together, and made us sit together in heavenly places in Christ Jesus:"

> **Ephesians 2:4-6**

Our position in Christ is "far above all principality, and power, and might and dominion..." [Ephesians 1:21]. Through our identification with Christ we have the same legal authority over the devil that Jesus has! That's what I John 4:17 says as it declares: "...as He (Jesus) is, so are we in this world."

We must remember, however, that the exercise of every being's authority is limited by the boundaries of its jurisdiction. Only within certain boundaries can the believer exercise his authority. Outside of these boundaries he cannot exercise authority. The authority of the believer has limitations that must be recognized. Let's identify some of the boundaries which determine the extent and limitations of the believer's authority.

## The Boundary of the Spirit Realm

II Corinthians 10:3-4 reveals a very important boundary that governs our authority as believers,

**"For though we walk in the flesh, we do not war after the flesh: For the weapons of our warfare are not carnal, but mighty through God to the pulling down of strongholds..."**

The true jurisdiction of the believer is in the realm of the spirit, for our authority is not a natural authority, but a spiritual authority.

II Corinthians 10:3 says, "For though we walk in the flesh, we do not war after the flesh." Our authority is not in the natural realm! Though our authority can be used to change circumstances in the physical realm, it is not from the physical realm that we operate or exercise our intervention. Our spiritual authority is exercised from our position in Christ. By using the weapons of preaching, prayer, confession, and other spiritual weapons, we fight our good fight of faith. Continuing on to verse four we read, "For the weapons of our warfare are not carnal...". If the weapons of our warfare are not carnal, then they must be spiritual!

To war after the flesh is to war outside the range of our authority. We step outside the jurisdiction of our authority when we resort to the natural weaponry of carnal man! But when we remain in that territory called the realm of the spirit we can exercise our right to intervene in the matters of this world.

### *Pulling Down Strongholds*

Politics have become a great concern in Christendom today. Never before have so many believers involved themselves in governmental affairs. While I truly believe that God is moving upon the hearts of many to stand up and declare what His Word has to say about the social concerns of our nations, I cannot help but wonder what would happen if that same amount of time, energy, and power were channeled through our jurisdiction in the spirit and directed through our weapon of prayer.

Our weapons, you see, are not picket lines or political parties. Our weapons are not manipulation, creative campaigning or the exertions of human abilities. Our weapons are the spiritual firearms of prayer, intercession, preaching, the name of Jesus and gifts of the Holy Ghost.

This is not meant to criticize those that involve themselves in the political scenes of their country. This is not to downgrade those who make public demonstrations declaring the righteous cause of Christ before the media and the masses of their cities. No, we as Christians are called to be the light of the world and the salt of the earth. To be such we are going to have to get out of our "shakers" and out into our world to perform the "curing" and "preserving" that salt is intended to do. However, mere marching and political parading alone will <u>never</u> pull down strongholds that can only come down as we "war after the spirit." It is only when we utilize the powerful weapons God has given us and operate in the spirit realm that we will obtain lasting results.

We must remember that our authority is not in the flesh, but in the spirit. Our weapons are not of the natural realm, but our weapons are a spiritual "firepower", full of God's ability! When we hook up with God's way of running our countries and step over into the "arena" of prayer, we will see a change come into the governments of the world!

James 5:16 says that, "...The effectual fervent prayer of a righteous man availeth much." Elijah, a man of like passions with us, stepped over into the spirit through the avenue of prayer and changed the condition of his nation! He did not resort to natural means, but operated within the boundaries of the realm of the spirit. In so doing he brought great physical change to the earth.

In Acts 12:5 "prayer was made without ceasing of the church unto God..." for the release of Peter from prison. The church did not boycott the king. They did not launch a protest or lobby for their cause. They stepped over into the jurisdiction where they could bring forth supernatural results and lifted up their voices in prayer. In response to that prayer Peter's circumstances where radically altered. An angel came and freed him from prison. Not only were Herod and his henchmen surprised, but even the church was surprised at the swift and amazing results which resulted from simply stepping over into the realm of the spirit and praying.

Paul told the church at Phillipi that he was confident that supernatural things would transpire when they exercised their authority in the realm of the spirit through prayer,

> **"For I know that this shall turn to my salvation through your prayer, and the supply of the Spirit of Christ."**

A man or woman may be insignificant in the natural realm, but authoritative and effectual in the spirit. Paul wrote in II Corinthians 5:16, "...henceforth know we no man after the flesh..." A person who is unimpressive in the natural can be very effectual when they step over into the realm of the spirit. When we realize the vast authority we have in the spirit, we will stop resorting to natural ways of warfare and step over into God's way of warfare!

I believe this is one thing Paul had in mind when he exhorted Timothy saying, "No man that warreth entangleth himself with the affairs of this life" [II Timothy 2:4]. He was encouraging Timothy not to entangle himself with the natural, carnal way of doing things. Our real authority and effectiveness does not rest in what we can do in the natural realm, but what we can do, "...through <u>God</u> to the pulling down of strongholds."

Even if there are two ways of accomplishing the same task, it is wisdom to use the most effective way. Why use a bow and arrow if you have a machine gun? Let's use our most lethal weapons; the weapons that work in the realm of the spirit.

It is when we step over into the realm of the spirit and pray that we can bring God's will to pass. It is when we use our spiritual weapons which are mighty through God that we can turn the hearts of our government leaders. Proverbs 21:1 declares, "The king's heart is in the hand of the Lord, as the rivers of water: he turneth it withersoever he (God) will." Because of your position in Christ, you have jurisdiction in the realm of the spirit. You don't necessarily need to be a spiritual giant or a seasoned veteran of prayer. Just put on your "badge" of authority, step into the spirit and begin to pray.

## The Boundary of Faith

The authority of the believer will not successfully operate outside the boundaries of faith. In the gospel of Matthew we find an account that illustrates this point,

> **"And when they were come to the multitude, there came to him a certain man, kneeling down to him, and saying, Lord, have mercy on my son: for he is a lunatick, and sore vexed: for ofttimes he falleth into the fire, and oft into the water. And I brought him to thy disciples, and they could not cure him. Then Jesus answered and said, O faithless and perverse generation, how long shall I be with you? how long shall I suffer you? bring him hither to me. And Jesus rebuked the devil; and he departed out of him: and the child was cured from that very hour. Then came the disciples to Jesus apart, and said, Why could not we cast him out? And Jesus said unto them, Because of your unbelief..."**

> **Matthew 17:14-20a**

Jesus had already delegated to the disciples authority to cast out devils. But this delegated authority would not function outside the boundary of faith. Though only a few weeks before Jesus had empowered the twelve with "...power over unclean spirits, to cast them out..." [Matthew 10:1], they failed to exercise their authority because they operated outside the boundary of faith. The fact that their authority over this particular demonic spirit was limited was a great surprise to these twelve men. Upon questioning Jesus, however, they discovered that their delegated authority would not operate outside the boundary of faith.

This account in Matthew reminds me of a story that Brother Kenneth E. Hagin tells in his book <u>I Believe in Visions</u>, in the chapter *"If — the Badge of Doubt."* In this chapter Brother Hagin recalls an instance in the early days of his healing ministry when he was attempting to cast a devil out of a man who had tuberculosis of the spine. After he cast the devil out of the sick man, Brother Hagin said to the man, "See <u>if</u> you can stoop over and bend your back." Brother Hagin recalls that as long as he asked the man to "See <u>if</u> you can...", the man could not. Jesus appeared to brother Hagin at this time and instructed him concerning this situation. Following this vision he made a correction and **commanded** the man to bend over in the name of Jesus. The man obeyed and was instantly healed. Brother Hagin concluded that chapter of his book by saying,

> *"I learned that no matter who we are, if we move in unbelief, we will stop the flow of God's power."*

I share this story to illustrate the fact that our authority as believers will not operate outside the boundary line of faith. Another way of expressing this truth is to say that we negate our authority when we step outside the boundary line of faith.

## The Boundary of the Fruit of the Spirit

After I awoke from my dream the Holy Spirit unfolded more and more principles to me from God's Word that relate to the law of Spiritual Jurisdiction. He took me to Galatians 5:16-23 which says,

> **"This I say then, Walk in the Spirit, and ye shall not fulfil the lust of the flesh. For the flesh lusteth against the Spirit, and the Spirit against the flesh: and these are contrary the one to the other: so that ye cannot do the things that ye would. But if ye be led of the Spirit, ye are not under the law. Now the works of the flesh are manifest, which are these; Adultery, fornication,**

uncleanness, lasciviousness, Idolatry, witchcraft, hatred, variance, emulations, wrath, strife, seditions, heresies, Envyings, murders, drunkenness, revellings, and such like: of the which I tell you before, as I have also told you in time past, that they which do such things shall not inherit the kingdom of God. But the fruit of the Spirit is love, joy, peace, longsuffering, gentleness, goodness, faith, Meekness, temperance: against such there is no law."

Here we find other boundary lines that define the ranges of authority in the two distinct and diametrically opposite kingdoms that co-exist and operate in the earth today. The boundaries of the kingdom of darkness are defined as the works of the flesh. The boundaries of the kingdom where Jesus is Lord are called the fruit of the spirit. The borders within which you live will determine how much authority you will be able to walk in.

Galatians 5:19-21 identifies several borders in Satan's jurisdiction and calls them the works of the flesh. As long as we walk within these borders we are subjecting ourselves to Satan and allowing him to lord it over our lives. You may say, "I am not subjecting myself to Satan's domain." But according to what we have already learned from Romans 6:16 you are! To whomever you yield yourselves to obey, to him you become a servant!

When we yield ourselves to serve the lust of the flesh we not only lower ourselves into Satan's jurisdiction, but we also forfeit our authority as believers. We place ourselves within the territory where he has the right to exercise his power and where we lose the right to exercise ours. When we walk in the works of the flesh we are <u>not</u> walking within the jurisdiction of the authority that God has given us.

The contrast is also true. When we walk in the spirit, then we <u>will not</u> walk within the dark borders of the lust of the flesh. When we walk in the fruit of the spirit we are free from Satan's authority not only legally, but in our actual daily walk. And most importantly our own authority can be exercised **fully** as we remain within the boundaries of the fruit of the spirit. Within these borders we can reign in life!

Galatians 5:23 says concerning these nine fruits of the spirit that, "...against such there is no law." W. E. Vine's Expository Dictionary of New Testament Words says that concerning the person living in the fruit of the spirit, or the believer that is led of the spirit that, "the law has no scope in his life...in so far as he is led by the spirit." Scope is another way of saying range, or jurisdiction. In other words, the death of the law has no jurisdiction in the life of the believer walking in the fruit of the spirit.

The fruit of the spirit represents a boundary line that defines the limitations and extent of our spiritual jurisdiction. Praise God, when we walk within the boundary lines of the fruit of the spirit, against these borders there is no jurisdiction of the devil or of sin at all. When a person truly walks in the fruit of the spirit not only is Satan's jurisdiction stopped, but he can exercise his authority in the realm of the unseen world!

## The Boundary Line of Love

One fruit of the spirit that marks the range of our jurisdiction more clearly than any other listed is the boundary line of love. Many fail to recognize what walking in love is really all about. Walking in love means to walk within the boundaries of God's jurisdiction as well as your own. When you walk within this jurisdiction God can bless you. When you walk in love you walk free from Satan's ability to destroy your life. When you walk in love you walk within that defined border where your own authority will fully operate. Your authority as a believer will not function beyond the border line of love! One step out of love is a step over the border line where your full authority is no longer intact.

One step outside of love is a step into darkness and a step into Satan's range of attack. One step out of love is one step away from the jurisdiction where God has the right to bless you with His best. God cannot bless us when we are in strife or when we are fighting with our brother or sister in the Lord.

Another way of stating this truth is to say that walking in love activates three areas of spiritual jurisdiction in our lives. First, walking in love keeps us in a place where God can bless us and give us what we need. Jesus taught that when we stand praying in faith for our needs, we must forgive the offenses of others before we are able to receive blessings from God [Mark 11:25-26].

Second, walking in love keeps us out of Satan's jurisdiction and his demonic chains of bondage. It was for this reason that Paul wrote to Timothy in II Timothy 2:24-26 and instructed that,

> "...the servant of the Lord must not strive, but be gentle unto all men, apt to teach, patient, In meekness instructing those that oppose themselves; if God peradventure will give them repentance to the acknowledging of the truth; And that they may recover themselves out of the snare of the devil, who are taken captive by him at his will."

Walking in love is walking in the light. The opposite of this is also true. Walking in unforgiveness or hatred is walking in darkness; outside of the light of God's Word. We forfeit our authority over the devil and actually are on his "turf" when we get into strife. When we walk in hatred, resentment, envy and quarreling then we enter into Satan's range of authority. We get into his jurisdiction. Whether we like it or not, when we are in the devil's jurisdiction we are in the region where he has the right to enforce his power. We are unprotected and without our authority. James 3:16 actually says, "for where envying and strife is, there is confusion and every evil work!"

We talk many times about "opening a door" to the devil, but a more accurate description would be to say that we actually "descend into his jurisdiction." We lower ourselves into the devil's domain by getting into strife and other works of the flesh; by not walking in love. Not only do we "give him place" as it says in Ephesians 4:27, but we actually "get into his place"; into the place where he has the right to enforce his power.

Third, walking in love keeps our authority and faith intact. Walking in love keeps our faith working [Galatians 5:6] and keeps our authority over Satan in force.

We see the importance of operating within the boundary lines of love by what John said in his first epistle,

> **"He that saith he is in the light, and hateth his brother, is in darkness even until now. He that loveth his brother abideth in the light, and there is none occasion of stumbling in him. But he that hateth his brother is in darkness, and walketh in darkness, and knoweth not whither he goeth, because that darkness hath blinded his eyes."**
>
> **I John 2:9-11**

The walk of love is a walk within the borders of our jurisdiction and will always keep our authority intact for "Love never fails" [I Corinthians 13:8].

## The Boundary of God's Word

The final boundary of the believers jurisdiction that we will look at is the boundary line of God's Word. Our authority only works within the confines of the written Word of God. We cannot exercise authority beyond the scriptures. People are operating in presumption and foolishness when they try to exercise authority beyond what the Bible teaches. But when we stay within the boundary of God's Word we can boldly and confidently stand in our position in Christ and enforce our authority.

A confirmation that the Word of God is a boundary line defining the range of our authority can be seen by what Jesus said in John 15:5. He told us, "Without me you can do nothing." We would be well within the laws of scriptural interpretation to say that outside of the Word we can do nothing. Outside of the Word of God we have no authority.

Our authority over Satan can only be exerted when we operate within the borderlines of God's Word. Even in the ministry of deliverance, if Satan can get you on his "turf" through unbelief, or if you go past the directions of God's Word, then you will not be able to cast out devils even though you have the legal authority to do so!

For example, those who try to cast devils out and command them to go to hell, or try to cast them into the abyss or the lake of fire, will not be able to successfully minister deliverance to the captives. That person is trying to operate their authority outside the boundaries of God's written Word. Nowhere does the Bible say that we can cast demons back into hell, or into the abyss or the lake of fire. No, the Bible simply says that we should cast demons out of those who are possessed. That's all we need to do.

Any time the devil can seduce us or deceive us over the boundary line of God's Word, our authority over him will be less effective and his operations will remain intact. Therefore, let's remain in the Word and, thereby, maintain our full authority as believers.

## Conclusion

There are boundary lines and limiting borders that define the range of authority or spiritual jurisdiction we have as believers. The boundaries of the realm of the spirit, of faith, of the fruit of the spirit, of the love of God, and of the Word of God are boundaries that define our jurisdiction. These are boundaries we must abide within if we expect to walk in the level of power that has been legally provided for us. When we transgress these boundary lines and leave the borders of our authority, we lose power in our lives and experience a breakdown in the true authority purchased for us by God. However, remaining within the boundary lines of our spiritual jurisdiction will enable us to fully appropriate the authority that does belong to us as believers.

# Spiritual Jurisdiction and the Ministry

## Chapter Eight

# Staying Within Your Calling

"But we will not boast of things without our measure, but according to the measure of the rule which God hath distributed to us, a measure to reach even unto you. For we stretch not ourselves beyond our measure, as though we reached not unto you: for we are come as far as to you also in preaching the gospel of Christ: Not boasting of things without our measure, that is, of other men's labours..."

**II Corinthians 10:13-15**

The Lord spoke very clearly to me when I awoke from my dream and said, "If one does not understand the principle of spiritual jurisdiction and realize that there are ranges of spiritual authority, he will have a very difficult time flowing with Me in these last days." You see, this principle of spiritual jurisdiction governs even the realm of ministry.

There are boundary lines that govern the scope of operation of every ministry gift and every ministry office. By ministry gift I mean every member of the body of Christ, for every member does have a ministry. By ministry office I am referring to the five-fold ministry gifts as specified in Ephesians 4:11. Ignorance or violation of the principle of Spiritual Jurisdiction as it relates to ministry has caused great grief in the kingdom of God and has even brought early death to some of God's great ministers. Violation of the principle of spiritual jurisdiction can wreak great havoc in the body of Christ.

## Borders in Ministry

We can learn some tremendous truths concerning jurisdiction in the ministry from the writings of Paul in II Corinthians 10:13,

> **"But we will not boast of the things without our measure, but according to the measure of the rule which God hath distributed to us, a measure to reach even unto you."**

Paul writes here of a definite region within which he had the right to operate and outside of which he had no right to operate. A look at some other translations of this scripture will help us see more clearly that there are jurisdictional borders that govern ministry. The New Testament in Modern Speech by Richard Weymouth translates II Corinthians 10:13 this way,

> **"We, however, will not boast beyond our due limits, but will keep within the limit of the field which God has assigned to us as a limit..."**

There are limits God assigns as a "field of ministry." He not only calls people to the ministry, but specifies boundary lines that define their callings. Just as a farmer might send a worker into a particular field to accomplish a specific task, so also does the Lord send ministers into particular fields to accomplish specific tasks. Ministers cannot do whatever they please, but must operate in subjection to the boundaries of their calling. God expects us to stay within the boundaries of our assignments and get the job done!

The Moffat translation renders II Corinthians 10:13 this way,

> **"And so my boasting never goes beyond the limit— it is determined by the limits of the sphere marked out for me by God..."**

Notice the phrase, "...the limits of the sphere marked out for me by God." "Sphere" means range of action. God marks out for ministers a range of operation; a jurisdiction of ministry. The New English Bible translates II Corinthians 10:13 this way,

> **"...and our sphere is determined by the limits that God has assigned us..."**

Our sphere of ministry is determined by the limits God has assigned to us. Or we could say: The limits of our assignments are determined by our callings. The boundaries of our jurisdiction are defined by the offices to which we are called and by the specific tasks we are given to accomplish. It is vitally important for ministers to know that they <u>have</u> a jurisdiction and to know <u>what</u> their jurisdiction is.

The Amplified Bible's translation of II Corinthians 10:13 clarifies the reality of these limits even more,

> **"We, on the other hand, will not boast beyond our legitimate province and proper limit, but will keep within the limits [of our commission which] God has allotted us as our measuring line..."**

The measuring line that defines the jurisdiction of a minister's activity is the commission God has given. In other words, the boundaries of your ministerial jurisdiction are determined by what God has called you to do. Your authority in ministry never goes beyond the boundaries of your God-given commission. You only have authority to carry out the task that you have been assigned to do. Outside of your calling you do not have the responsibility or the right to exercise any authority.

Ministers must remain within their jurisdictions not only in order to effectively complete the tasks God has given them, but also to avoid the mistake of encroaching upon another man's God-given assignment. We must stay within the boundaries of the commission and calling God has placed upon our lives. If He has called us to do a particular task, then let's perform that task. But let's not step outside our commission.

## Staying in Your Lane

Every ministry gift and calling from God has boundary lines and limits of responsibility that must be recognized and strictly adhered to. Ministers have been given responsibilities and, therefore, have authority to carry out those responsibilities. But just as responsibilities are limited by calling, so also authority is limited by calling. This is what Spiritual Jurisdiction is all about. It is about understanding that there is a range of spiritual authority which governs spiritual operation.

Paul wrote in II Corinthians 10:13,

> **"...but according to the measure of the rule which God hath distributed to us..."**

A study of the words *"measure"* and *"rule"* will clarify further the fact that there are boundaries in the ministry within which we must work. The word translated measure is the Greek word *"metron"* and the word translated rule is the Greek word *"kanon."* These words were used by Paul to describe the boundary lines of his ministry. Finis J. Dake in his study Bible makes this comment about II Corinthians 10:13,

> *"Here Paul seems to be using the figure of a stadium or race course in the Olympic and Isthmian games. The metron [measure] was the length of the dromos [course], and the kanon [rule] was the same as the white line that marked the boundaries of the stadium."*

Paul often used athletic events to illustrate spiritual truths. There is little doubt that he is doing the same here.

The metron [measure] can be understood as the length of one's ministry course and the kanon [rule] as the boundaries of one's lane. No matter what one's ministry gift or commission, no matter how far God has called one to run, each must stay in their own lane! Whether God has called you to run a 100 yard dash or a 26 mile marathon you need to stay in your lane and not cross the white line that defines the boundaries of your course!

Irrespective of your ministerial office, whether you are called to be an apostle, a prophet, a pastor, a teacher or an evangelist, you must stay within the boundaries of your own course and out of the "lane" of another man's office. What Vine's says about the word "kanon" reinforces the importance of staying within your lane,

> *"Here it [kanon] specifies the limits of responsibility in gospel service as measured and appointed by God."*

Note very carefully that whether or not you finish the *metron* [length] of your course will be determined by your endurance. But whether or not you stay within the *kanon* [boundary line] of your course is determined by your obedience to the law of Spiritual Jurisdiction!

## Don't Step Out of Bounds

Let's go back to II Corinthians 10 and study some more things about staying in our lane from the fourteenth verse,

> **"For we stretch not ourselves beyond our measure, as though we reached not unto you; for we are come as far as to you also in preaching the gospel of Christ:"**

By saying, "For we stretch not ourselves beyond our measure...", Paul is addressing a very real possibility. It is possible to go beyond what God has given you as an assignment and, thereby, go beyond your spiritual jurisdiction as a minister. A look at the language Paul uses from some other translations will further illustrate the need to be careful about stepping out of our lane. The Amplified Bible says,

> **"For we are not overstepping the limits of our province (territory)..." [parenthesis mine]**

Again, the implication here is that it is possible for a minister to overstep the limits of what God has called him to do. Moffat's translation says,

> **"I am not overstepping the limit, as if you lay beyond my sphere..."**

The Knox translation says,

> **"Nobody can say that we are encroaching..."**

No one could say that Paul was encroaching on another man's labors because he stayed within the boundaries of his own commission. It is essential that ministers and ministries do not trespass the limits of their own jurisdiction and, thus, encroach upon another man's ministry. Other translations of II Corinthians 10:4 say,

**"We are not over stretching our commission..."** *NEB*

**"For I am not overstepping my authority..."**
**Williams Translation**

**"We are not going too far..."** *Taylor*

All these translations emphasize the reality that with every calling from God come boundaries which define both the range of responsibility and the range of authority. If Paul was careful to stay within the limits of his ministry responsibility, how much more should we pay attention and stay within the boundaries of our own spiritual jurisdiction in ministry.

Within our limits of responsibility is our work and our jurisdiction. Outside the limits of our responsibility is someone else's work and jurisdiction. Within the boundaries of our calling and labor is our jurisdiction. To step outside the boundaries of our jurisdiction is to transgress into another man's calling and labor. Ministers who through ignorance consistently transgress the borders of their ministerial rights and authority cause much grief to the kingdom of God.

It is important to understand what God has called you to do and to stay within the boundaries and limits of your assignment. II Timothy 2:5 says,

**"And if a man also strive for the masteries, yet is he not crowned, except he strive lawfully."**

Again Paul is comparing the life of ministry to an Olympic contest. If a man competes in a contest he will only be rewarded if he competes lawfully. W. E. Vine notes that this word lawfully [Gr. *nominos*] is an adverb used to describe the action of running a race. Vine states, "In II Timothy 2:5 it [*nominos*] is used of contending in the games and adhering to the rules." The race Paul is talking about is our course of ministry on earth. Stepping outside the boundary lines of our responsibilities may not always result in calamity here on earth, but <u>will</u> certainly disqualify us for the rewards that are to be passed out in the life to come.

To many, success in ministry is perceived as nothing more than success in this life. Some ministers operate outside the boundaries of their callings for years, but because they do not see any immediate negative consequences falsely conclude that what they are doing is alright. Ministry, however, is more than just a life of success for today. There are eternal rewards we should be striving for that will be passed out in the life to come! There can also be eternal losses, however, if we fail to lawfully complete the specific ministry which the Lord has assigned to us. It is for this reason that we must stay within the boundaries of our callings, contending according to the rules of God's Word and according to the commission He has given us.

## Chapter Nine

# Surveying Your Borders

**"As every man hath received the gift, even so minister the same one to another, as good stewards of the manifold grace of God."**

**I Peter 4:10**

In chapter eight we learned that the law of Spiritual Jurisdiction governs the operation of ministry gifts and ministry offices. We learned that every ministry gift and ministry office has a jurisdiction which both authorizes and limits their sphere of oversight and operation in the body of Christ. We emphasized the importance of staying within the limits of your commission and within the boundary lines of the responsibilities God has delegated to you. In this chapter we will ask some questions to help you determine the borders of your own ministry and share with you some attitudinal guidelines you should follow as you ask these questions.

The answers to these important questions will help you assess the borders of your own jurisdiction. Operating within your own borders will authorize you to confidently minister and enjoy God's anointing. Operating outside your borders may jeopardize your life and ministry and cause problems for those to whom you minister.

## Eight Questions To Help You Determine Your Borders

### Question 1:
### Am I called to the fivefold ministry?

The first and foremost question to ask yourself as you

determine the borders of your activity in ministry is, "Am I called to the five-fold ministry"?

Every member in the body of Christ has a ministry. Every child of God has a function in the church. No matter how big or small you may feel, no matter how important or insignificant you may perceive yourself to be, the body needs you and will only be successful if you fulfill your role. No one who is born again is without a calling to do their part, and no one who has been saved has been placed into the body without having been given a gift for service. Romans 12:4-5 says,

> "For as we have many members in one body, and all members have not the same office (Gr. function). So we, being many, are one body in Christ, and every one members one of another."

In this passage we see that just as the physical body is made up of different parts, but every part has a function, so it is true of the body of Christ. We all have a function, or ministry, as a member of the body of Christ. I Peter 4:10 says that,

> "As every man hath received the gift, even so minister the same one to another, as good stewards of the manifold grace of God."

Though everyone has a <u>gift</u> for service in the body of Christ, however, not everyone holds an <u>office</u> in the church. Because this is true, not everyone has the same level of authority. Though everyone in the body is of equal importance, not everyone is of equal authority. For though everyone has a ministry gift that they should use to build the church, not all are called to ministry offices. A ministry gift is different from a ministry office. All have been given gifts, but not all have been called to stand in a ministry office.

There are differing levels of grace imparted by God to carry out different callings. Romans 12:6 says,

> "Having then gifts differing according to the grace that is given to us..."

The answer to this first question, "Am I called to a fivefold office?" is not meant to reveal your degree of importance in the body of Christ, but to reveal your degree of responsibility and authority by virtue of the responsibility and authority given those in the fivefold offices.

If you are called to one of the very important ministries of helps, then you will have a specific jurisdiction within which you function in the body. However, you will not carry the same level of authority as one of the eldership positions of overseeing God's sheep as represented by the fivefold ministry offices. You should never be disappointed, however, if you are not called to a fivefold ministry office. In all actuality, you should rejoice that you can serve the Lord so heartily without the great accountability of those offices. James 3:1 from the NIV says this,

> **"Not many of you should presume to be teachers, my brothers, because you know that we who teach will be judged more strictly."**

This question, "Am I called to the fivefold ministry?", is the first question you need to ask yourself as you determine the boundaries of your responsibility and authority in the church and in ministry. The questions that follow, though they seem somewhat more directed to those who know they are called to the fivefold ministry, are applicable to all believers.

## Question Two:
## What ministry am I called to?

This second question, perhaps more than any other, will help you identify <u>what</u> you are *authorized* to do and *limited* to in your ministry. The basic God-given job description and duties of each office act as border lines that define the jurisdiction of each ministry.

If, for example, you are called to pastor a church then you know that you will be authorized and anointed to feed and oversee a local flock of believers. You would not, however, be authorized or anointed to operate as a travelling ministry or in any other office outside the pastorate God has given you. If you are called to the ministry of helps, then your function and jurisdiction will not include the right to govern a local church. If you are a travelling teacher who ministers from local church to local church you will not have the jurisdiction to correct congregational problems in a local body. Though you may have the right to clarify doctrine through your gift of teaching, you should not "take it upon yourself" to intervene into matters that clearly fall within the responsibility of that local pastor.

A good Bible example of a man who stayed within the borders of his calling can be found in Acts 8:5-25. Philip the Evangelist was mightily used of God to bring revival to the city of Samaria. He operated within the jurisdiction of his evangelistic office and preached Christ to them. Many were won to the Lord and great miracles were performed among the people. Though multitudes were saved and baptized, however, Philip did not transgress the borders of his calling and try to be something that he was not. He did not assume another man's responsibility in ministering the baptism in the Holy Ghost. Though Philip was filled with the Holy Ghost himself [Acts 6:3-5] and could have ministered the infilling of the Spirit to those Samaritan believers, he passed that ministry activity over to the apostles who were authorized by the Lord to minister the infilling of the Holy Spirit through the laying on of hands.

Today there are many individuals trespassing offices and going beyond the limits of their calling. They could learn a great lesson from Philip and quit trying to operate in things that they have not been assigned to do. Just because you can do something does not mean that you should. Just because you are able to minister a certain way does not mean that you have heaven's authorization to do so.

## Question Three:
### *What is the Purpose of My Call?*

Within the same office there can be different purposes. Two individuals may be called to the same office, but have different tasks they are to accomplish within that common office. For example, two different individuals may be called to the office of the teacher, but one may be assigned to act as a "front-runner", introducing certain truths to people, while the other may have the assignment of establishing people in truth they already know. The apostle Paul made this point when he contrasted his ministry with that of Apollos. He said that one planted and the other watered [I Corinthians 3:6]. Though two individuals may be called to the same office, and though they may teach the exact same Bible lessons, the purpose of their commission may be different.

This reality that the same offices can have different purposes can be illustrated from my own life and ministry. In the spring of 1979 I became fully aware of the ministry office I would begin in. At that time the Lord not only called me to the office of the teacher [and later as a pastor], but spoke specifically to me about the main purpose of my call. As I was reading Ephesians chapter four from the New International Version, I came to verses 11 and 12 which say,

> **"It was he who gave some to be apostles, some to be prophets, some to be evangelists, and some to be pastors and teachers. To prepare God's people for works of service, so that the body of Christ may be built up."**

As I read these verses God spoke to me as clearly as He ever has and called me into the fivefold ministry with the specific purpose of preparing God's people for works of service. As I read that verse the Holy Ghost spoke on the inside of me and said, "That's you, that's you, that's you." Without a shadow of a doubt I knew that was me. I knew then, and have continued to know, that the main purpose of my ministry as a pastor and teacher is to prepare God's people for works of service. My main purpose even as a pastor is to train and to prepare believers for their ministry in the body of Christ. Sure, there are many other duties I must perform in fulfilling the responsibilities of the shepherd's office, but the main thrust of my commission is to train and mobilize believers for their ministries.

Certainly Ephesians 4:12 is the general purpose of all the fivefold ministry gifts, and yet this is a specific commission and objective that I have been given. This commission constitutes a border within which I am authorized to minister and within which I must stay. I would be transgressing my jurisdiction to do anything else. Some pastors and churches have evangelism as the main thrust of their ministry. Others may have different specific thrusts of ministry that God has given them.

Another truth along these same lines is the fact that God often calls different churches within the same city to do different things. The call of God upon local churches can be different based upon the purpose for which God has raised that church up. Though the two ministries are both local churches and have local pastors and local believers, the purpose and, therefore, the thrust of the two churches may be different. Rather than these two local churches trying to be <u>like</u> each other, or even trying to be "all things to all men," they should pursue to the fullest the purpose for which God has commissioned them.

Some churches know that their main purpose is missions. Some churches have been commissioned to minister to the down and out. I personally know a pastor who is supernaturally endowed with an anointing to love and nurture baby Christians. After they get on their feet spiritually they move on to other local churches where they can grow further in the things of God and fulfill the ministry calling that is upon their lives. It is as if God has assigned that pastor and local church to be a "spiritual nursery" in the kingdom of God.

Certainly every church should prepare the saints, involve themselves in evangelism and missions, minister to the poor, and nurture spiritual babies. But beyond the general duties of ministries and ministry offices there are specific purposes and main thrusts that God assigns even to those who may hold the same offices.

In surveying your boundary lines you must not only ask the question, "What ministry gift am I called to fulfill?", but,

"What is the main purpose I am to accomplish within the borders of that ministry?" I believe this is part of what the Lord meant in I Corinthians 12:5-6,

**"And there are difference of administrations (ministries), but the same Lord. And there are diversity of operations, but it is the same God which worketh all in all." [parenthesis mine]**

Notice verse five says that there are different kinds of ministries. That is something we have recognized for years. But verse six goes on to say that there are also "diversity of operations." This word "operations" is the Greek word *"energema."* W. E Vine says this word means, "what is wrought, the effect produced by...." In other words, there can be different effects produced by individuals that stand in the same office. The effect produced by one evangelist may be different than the effect produced by another evangelist. Though they are both called to the office of the evangelist, their specific purpose in ministry is different. Because their purpose is different, their effect in ministry will be different. We can, therefore, locate another boundary of our office and our operation by asking the question, "What is the purpose of my calling?"

## *Question Four:*
### *Do I have a specific message?*

A look at some possible answers to this question will further help you to survey the borders of your ministerial jurisdiction. Ask yourself, "What am I called to preach?", or "What am I called to teach or share?" Certainly God has called all of us to preach the Word. But sometimes God assigns specific messages to specific individuals. If He does so, then that assignment must be adhered to. If God were to tell you to, "Go teach my people healing", then that should be the message you stick with until otherwise directed by the Holy Ghost. If the Lord were to commission you to teach about the family, then you must abide within that call. That does not mean that there would never be exceptions to your commission or times when the Lord might have you minister a timely message to a special group. But by and large you should focus upon and stay within the borders of that commission.

This important lesson, along with many other valuable lessons, can be learned from brother Kenneth E. Hagin. He has always stayed within his assignment. When God told him to, "Go teach my people faith", then brother Hagin preached on faith. When God said, "Stay in the churches", then brother Hagin stayed in the churches. You know, it is amazing how blessings come our way when we simply obey the commission that God has allotted our life. Find out if God has called you to preach a specific message and preach it. For those of you who are pastors, your general assignment is to preach a well balanced diet; all the Word. But for others who travel from place to place, from church to church, this question may prove very valuable in determining your jurisdiction.

## *Staying Within the Borders of God's Word*

Along with this guideline question of, "What am I called to preach?", would certainly be the importance of staying within the boundaries of sound doctrine. Our authority as ministers does not extend beyond the borders of sound doctrine. Though this truth seems to be self-evident, today it needs to be said loud and clear. Though a teacher has authority to teach, he does not have the authority to teach things that are not in the Bible. It seems ridiculous that one would have to address this at all, but many are crossing outside this boundary line and preaching false doctrine. Doctrines which may sound very "spiritual" and full of excitement, but do not fall within the borders of solid scriptural truth.

In the previous chapter I referred to Paul's use of the Olympic games in II Corinthians 10:13-14 in defining areas of spiritual jurisdiction in the ministry. There I stressed the importance of staying within your lane and not encroaching upon another man's course or office. In addressing this border of sound doctrine I want to encourage you to be very careful to remain on the right track. Some have not only left their lane, but they aren't even running in the right stadium! By preaching things that are not Biblically sound they not only jeopardize themselves, but also jeopardize those to whom they preach. For this reason Paul wrote to Timothy and said,

> **"Take heed unto thyself, and unto the doctrine; continue in them; for in doing this thou shalt save both thyself, and them that hear thee."**
>
> **I Timothy 4:16**

I know that staying within the boundary lines of sound doctrine is a basic of ministry jurisdiction, but it is these basics that we need to practice the most.

## Question Five:
### Who am I called to serve?

Another question that will help you survey your borders is, "Who am I called to serve?" This question can apply to those who travel as well as to local pastors. God certainly calls ministers to certain groups of people. Sometimes He calls them to a certain nation; sometimes a certain race. This can be clearly illustrated by comparing the two apostolic offices of Peter and Paul. Galatians 2:8 says,

> **"(For he that wrought effectually in Peter to the apostleship of the circumcision, the same was mighty in me toward the Gentiles:)"**

Here we see that one's spiritual jurisdiction in the ministry can be limited by the call to serve a specific group or race of people. Paul was an apostle to the Gentiles, but his jurisdiction did not extend unto the Jews. Peter's jurisdiction extended unto the Jews, but his ministry did not cross the borders unto the Gentiles. One time Peter ministered to the house of Cornelius [a Gentile] on a temporary assignment because he had specific instructions from God. Because God told him to go, he had the authority to go and an anointing to minister. After completing that specific assignment Peter went back to Jerusalem and we have no record that he ever went back among the Gentiles to preach. His main calling and range of responsibility was among the Jews. A special group of people can be limited to race, age [eg. children, youth, singles, etc], or other specific and specialized categories and classes of people. George Mueller, the English minister, was specifically called to minister to orphans.

It is very important that ministers recognize that just because they are called and given authority to oversee one group of people does not mean that they have jurisdiction over other groups. Just because one is called as an apostle to one nation does not mean that he can exert apostolic rights or authority "carte blanche" over another nation. Standing in the office of the apostle in one country does not authorize one to stand in that office in another country.

Trying to enforce one's ministry authority over anyone is a wrong attitude in the first place. However, attempting to exert one's ministry authority in an area or among a people that are not a <u>direct</u> <u>fruit</u> of one's ministry efforts is a violation of spiritual jurisdiction.

This spiritual violation is often seen among those who call themselves "apostles", or who may really be called as apostles, but attempt to operate outside this boundary of, "Who am I called to serve?" Such are those who approach an already established church and attempt to bring the local pastor and church body under his control. This person may attempt to enforce his authority over that church based upon the office he says he is called to. However, one's jurisdiction does not extend unto those they have had no direct role in raising up and nurturing.

By "direct role in raising up and nurturing" of a local church I mean more than just an endorsement of the local pastor or an occasional visit in that pulpit. It was because Paul had been the first to preach the gospel of Christ to the Corinthians and was the one who "gave birth" to that work that he could exercise authority concerning the church in Corinth. II Corinthians 10:14 says,

**"For we stretch not ourselves beyond our measure, as though we reached not unto you: for we are come as far to you also in preaching the gospel of Christ:"**

A man who attempts by force or intimidation to take the oversight of an already established work, a work that is not the fruit of his labors, is anything but a minister of the gospel. Furthermore any pastor who would permit such a thing to occur among his flock is anything but a true shepherd. Answering this question, "Who am I called to serve?", is a vital key to staying within one's ministry jurisdiction.

## *Question Six:*
## *Where am I called to serve?*

Sometimes even natural boundary lines such as countries, cities, or states may act as the defining borders of one's jurisdiction in the ministry. Certainly this would be the case of one sent by the Holy Ghost as a missionary to a specific country or of a pastor called to a local community. For example, a man sent by the Holy Ghost to the nation of Brazil would stand in a position of responsibility to that nation and, therefore, have authority and jurisdiction to minister there with the anointing. Though he may preach outside those geographic boundaries, his main duty and the jurisdiction of his ministry will predominately be within Brazil.

Likewise a pastor who is called to a local community may certainly preach and teach outside those city limits and be a blessing to the body of Christ. But the main thrust of his ministry activity will remain within the boundary lines of that community; among those to whom he was sent. I know personally that even though I have preached with an anointing in other pulpits outside our city, the greatest manifestation of my gift is within our own church. There have even been times when I have been out of town for a while that when I cross our county line and into the city limits of our local church, I feel the anointing of the Holy Spirit rest on me like a cloak.

Answering this question, "Where am I called to serve?", is also important for travelling ministers. If the Lord specifically assigned a travelling minister to the churches of the United States, simply satisfying his own whims to travel to to other countries will most likely result in problems in those overseas churches. Through violation of his assigned jurisdiction, he will become susceptible to deception and may deceive those to whom he ministers. When individuals go beyond the boundaries of God's will for their lives, they step beyond His ability to bless and protect. This great danger of stepping out beyond the will of God is part of what God was teaching me in my dream.

You will recall from my dream that it was not until I made it back into the territory that represented God's will that He was able to help me and that the demonic spirits had to stop their pursuit. I'm sure all of us can think of times when we went beyond what God had told us to do and experienced failure in ministry and life. It is because men *add to* or *take away from* the specific instructions of God that they miss out on his best for their lives and even suffer loss and undue difficulty.

Answering this question, "Where am I called to serve", is important in properly flowing with the law of spiritual jurisdiction.

### Seven:
### *How am I called to serve?*

The question, "How am I called to serve?" or, "How do I fulfill my calling?", will further define your jurisdiction in ministry. What mediums of communication did <u>God</u> call you to use and which one's did <u>you</u> choose?

Did you know that God will pay for what He commissions? Many financial disasters occur because individuals go beyond the boundary lines of what God called them to do. Of course there will be challenges even when we are in the perfect will of God. There will be times when the enemy attacks and we will have to fight the good fight of faith. But a constant struggle and a forever "red sea" of debt should send the gospel worker back to the prayer closet to see if he got all his instructions **correct**. How did God call you to minister? Did he really call you to television, or radio, or to write books? Did God really call you to have a Bible school or Christian day school?

Violating the boundary lines of, "How am I called to serve", has undoubtedly indebted many ministries. Don't be guilty of wanting to do something just because everyone else is doing it. Trying to be like everyone else is wrong in the first place. But getting involved in an area of ministry just because it is in "vogue" or the hot new thing to do is even more dangerous. I know a pastor whose very large church has dwindled to less than a third of what he had just a few years ago. The reason is because he tried to get on the bandwagon of every new thing that came along. He got outside of what God had called him to do by trying to be like everyone else and lost what God had blessed him with. He thinks God has "purged" his church. But if the truth be known, he has allowed the devil to steal his sheep by getting out where he did not belong. God's Word says that the Lord <u>added</u> people to the church daily, not that he took people away.

## *Question Eight:*
### *When am I called to serve?*

Some of the boundary lines we have studied up to this point are fairly obvious. There is, however, a boundary line which defines our jurisdiction in the ministry that may not be so obvious. That boundary line is time. So we must ask the question, "When am I called to serve?"

In the kingdom of God timing is essential; in fact, it can be everything. Not only do we need to soberly assess the what, the who, the way and the how of our calling, but we must answer the important question of, "When?" Answering this question will identify for you another border in your range of ministry.

The fact that time is a boundary in the law of spiritual jurisdiction can be recognized by examining the jurisdiction of Satan. As we established previously, Satan operates within his range of authority as the "prince of the power of the air." Though he is presently the ruler of the darkness, his rights of authority are limited to a span of time. In II Corinthians 4:4 Satan is called the "god of this world." The word "world" is the Greek word *"aion"* which, more literally translated, means "age." W. E. Vines Expository Dictionary of New Testament Words says that one definition of the word *"aion"* is, "a period of time."

Satan is the god of this age, or of this period of time. His authority in this world system will not be forever. It is limited to a specific span of time that was a part of the stewardship God delegated to Adam. You may recall that when Jesus entered the country of Gergesenes He was met by a demon possessed man. The demons in the man asked Jesus, "Art thou come hither to torment us before the time?" [Matthew 8:29] The demons know that there is a time when they will be tormented. Before that time, however, they are free from their impending torment and have rights, along with Satan, to torment on this earth.

God also has a time frame within which He operates. Though Jesus was "...the Lamb slain from the foundation of the world..." [Revelation 13:8], He was not sent to the earth to complete His commission until the "...fullness of time was come..." [Galatians 4:4] I Timothy 2:6 says that, "(Jesus) gave Himself a ransom for all, to be testified in due time." God works His plan within the time table He has designed. He moves very strategically, not just responding to emergencies. Though the children of Israel were suffering in great pain under the oppressive rule of Egypt, God did not send Moses before it was the appointed time. Though God meets all the personal needs in our lives, when it comes to His redemptive plan He has a time table and a design that He will adhere to.

This boundary line of time is critical in assessing the scope of our ministries. The reason some experience failure in ministry is because they get out ahead of God's timing. Though they have been commissioned to a particular task, they transgress the borders of God's timing and try to operate in an area of authority and anointing before it has been conferred upon them. The result of this mistake will inevitably be failure. Some people have a hard time in ministry because they try to kick down doors before the time God has designed that they should open. Moses certainly experienced difficulty by taking matters into His own hands and slaying the Egyptian [Exodus 7:11-15]. Likewise Sarah gave birth to a great conflict when she got ahead of God and sent her servant Hagar into Abraham to conceive a child [Genesis 16].

Another clear example of the boundary line of time can be seen in the life and ministry of the apostle Paul. Jesus met him on the road to Damascus in Acts 9:1-9 and, at that time, called him into the ministry. Three days later Ananias went to restore Paul's sight and more was revealed to Paul concerning his commission [Acts 9:10-13]. It was not, however, till many years later, in Acts 13:1-4, that Paul was actually sent forth by the Holy Ghost into the fullness of the work that God had already called him to.

## *Special Increments of Time*

It is important to understand that sometimes God may commission someone to do an assignment, but only for a small segment of time. When God gives a short term assignment it does not mean that that person has the right or authority to ever do that again. For example, God used Peter to go to the house of Cornelius and preach to the Gentiles on a special occasion, but Peter was not from then on called of God to minister to the Gentiles. Zacharias, the father of John the Baptist, prophesied under the anointing of the Holy Ghost about things to come, but that did not mean that he was a prophet from that point on. We must understand that although God may authorize us to minister in a particular fashion one time it does not mean that we have the jurisdiction to operate that way again.

Missing God's perfect timing is another area to watch for concerning violating spiritual jurisdiction in the ministry.

Let us walk ever so accurately in these last days and operate safely and boldly within the protective boundaries of the God given jurisdiction that is defined by our true ministries. Let us walk well within those borders and we will truly be walking with God.

## Chapter Ten

# Guidelines For Surveying
# Your Borders

*"For I say, through the grace given unto me, to every*
*man that is among you, not to think of himself more*
*highly than he ought to think; but to think soberly as*
*God hath dealt to every man the measure of faith."*

**Romans 12:3**

W hy do individuals overstep the boundaries of their God-given jurisdictions? Sometimes it is because they are thinking more highly of themselves than they ought to think. In Romans 12:3 we are exhorted to soberly and realistically assess our function in the body of Christ. We are challenged to examine the grace, or the distribution, that we have.

When one thinks more highly of himself than he ought the first thing that becomes blurred and obscure is the boundary lines of his ministry office. It is because of the deceiving power of spiritual pride that many attempt to operate beyond the true call of God upon their lives. Some think more highly of themselves than they ought to think because they do have the talents, resources, and abilities or even the knowledge to perform certain ministry tasks. But mere ability or even knowledge is no substitute for actually being called and anointed of God. Some have certain things in their hearts to do, but until they are commissioned and authorized from heaven to perform that task, they would do well to abide within their jurisdiction. We need to accurately evaluate what our ministry gift is and contentedly operate within the borders of that call.

A picture from the book of Ezekiel will illustrate this point of stepping out beyond God's call. In Ezekiel 47:1-5 we read that there issued out a great river of water from the heavenly temple,

> "Afterward he brought me again unto the door of the house; and, behold, waters issued out from under the threshold of the house eastward: for the forefront of the house stood toward the east, and the waters came down from under from the right side of the house, at the south side of the altar. Then brought he me out of the way of the gate northward, and led me about the way without unto the utter gate by the way that looketh eastward; and, behold, there ran out waters on the right side. And when the man that had the line in his hand went forth eastward, he measured a thousand cubits, and he brought me through the waters; the waters were to the ankles. Again he measured a thousand, and brought me through the waters; the waters were to the knees. Again he measured a thousand, and brought me through; the waters were to the loins. Afterward he measured a thousand; and it was a river that I could not pass over: for the waters were risen, waters to swim in, a river that could not be passed over."

Ezekiel observed this river, but he was not allowed to step in until it was measured out. Though the waters continued to deepen, he was not allowed to step out any deeper until it was measured for him to do so. This passage is not necessarily teaching spiritual jurisdiction, but it does give us a picture of not stepping out beyond what God has allotted. People do not need to step out in things of the ministry just because they want to. Stepping out in ministry is not something that we decide of our own volition. God must call before we can answer.

The reason some have such a hard time in the ministry is because they try to "kick down" doors that God has not opened before them. One cannot undertake a ministry assignment just because he wants to do it. In Acts 8:18-25 Simon desired to have the ministry of laying on of hands, but he was rebuked for supposing he could obtain an area of ministry just because he wanted it. We must be very careful about launching into an area of ministry just because we want to.

## Accurately Assessing Your Borders

Another scripture which challenges us in assessing our area of ministry is found in Galatians 6:3-4. It says,

**"For if a man think himself to be something, when he is nothing, he deceiveth himself. But let every man prove his own work, and then shall he have rejoicing in himself alone, and not in another."**

Romans 12:3 exhorted us to soberly survey what God has called us to do and not to be high minded in our evaluation. Galatians 6:3-4 teaches us to prove our own works; to examine our results. In our evaluating our range of spiritual authority and ministerial responsibility, let us not deceive ourselves into thinking we are more than what we really are. What we are producing is an indication of what our place in ministry is.

For example, if you are producing on a regular basis the fruit of multiple salvations, and great numbers of souls are saved each time you preach, that would seem to indicate that you have an evangelist's anointing. If through your presentation of the Word of God people are greatly blessed and grow in the Lord, then you may quite likely be called to the teaching ministry.

If, however, the fruit of your ministry is confusion and division, and if church splits and insubordination follow you, then your own fruit condemns you and judges that you have crossed over the limits of your commission and you have transgressed the boundaries of your spiritual jurisdiction.

Do not evaluate your borders by what you dream of becoming in the future, or by what you wish were true. But accurately survey your range of authority by the realities of what you have been given and by what you are producing. Soberly determine your call and stay within that race alone. Even if you see a need in the body of Christ, understand that the realization of a need does not constitute a calling. You must wait on the Lord. He may send you or He may send someone else that He has chosen for that task.

Do not take it upon yourself to do things that you think are good to do. More important than doing a <u>good</u> thing is doing <u>God's</u> thing. In soberly evaluating your borders, it would be better to sell yourself a little short and be conservative than to step out too far through pride and go beyond the limits of your call.

## Learn to be Content

Another attitude that causes individuals to transgress boundaries of gifts and offices is discontentment. Many want to step out in new things because they have become bored with the old. Some want to be great because they are discontent with being ordinary and plain. But I Corinthians 12:18 says that,

> "...God hath set the members, every one of them in the body, as it hath pleased him."

We are not in this world to please ourselves, but to please God. When we function in the place that God has set us with a knowledge that we are pleasing God, we <u>will</u> experience satisfaction.

Perceiving yourself as unimportant because you are not well known means that you don't have an appreciation or an understanding of the need for every member in the body of Christ. Paul stated in I Corinthians 12:15 that,

> "If the foot shall say, Because I am not the hand, I am not of the body; is it therefore not of the body?"

We need to do whatever God has called us to do and be content to stay in the place that God has put us. We should not change from one place to the next just because we need a change of scenery. No, we need to be content working in the field God has assigned us to and serve the Lord with gladness, rejoicing that He has assigned us to that task.

## Obedience is Better Than Sacrifice

While desiring to do something great for God may be noble, going beyond the will of God for your life and ministry can be very costly. Extending the borders of your commission of your own volition has cost some men their ministries. King Saul made this mistake. He desired to make a great sacrifice for God. The only problem was that God did not want Saul to give Him any great presents or gifts. Samuel said,

> **"...Hath the Lord as great delight in burnt offerings and sacrifices, as in obeying the voice of the Lord? Behold to obey is better than sacrifice, and to hearken than the fat of rams. For rebellion is as the sin of witchcraft, and stubbornness is as iniquity and idolatry. Because thou has rejected the word of the Lord, he has also rejected thee from being king."**

> **I Samuel 15:22**

Saul was rejected because he always had a better idea than God. Ministers run the risk of losing their anointing by going beyond their callings. David, in contrast with Saul, had this testimony,

> **"...I have found David the son of Jesse, a man after mine own heart, which shall fulfil all my will."**

> **Acts 13:22**

Fulfilling all of God's will, but doing no more and no less than what He has called you to do, is the greatest gift you can give to the Lord. It is the person who will stay within the boundary lines of obedience that God is looking for and that God can bless. These words of the prophet Hanani will encourage us to submit our will to God's will,

> **"For the eyes of the Lord run to and fro throughout the whole earth, to shew himself strong on the behalf of them whose heart is perfect toward him."**

> **II Chronicles 16:9**

## Minding Your Own Business

Paul, in addressing the principle of spiritual jurisdiction in II Corinthians 10, said in the 15th verse,

**"Not boasting of things without (outside) our measure, that is, of other men's labors..." [parenthesis mine]**

I like the Basic English's translation of this scripture,

**"Not taking credit to ourselves for what is not our business, that is, for the work of others..."**

Paul recognized that there were areas of ministry that were not his business. We, too, need to learn this. When we get busy trying to take care of every one else's business, we neglect taking care of our own. When we try to do what we are not called to do, we fail to accomplish the work that we are called to do. When we try to run someone else's race, we fail to run with patience the one that is set before us [Hebrews 12:1]. Learn to mind your own business and in so doing stay within your own ministry jurisdiction!

## Marching in Order

There is a picture in the book of Joel of an army of great power. One of the greatest attributes of this army is found in chapter 2:7-8,

**"They shall run like mighty men; they shall climb the wall like men of war; and they shall march every one on his ways, and they shall not break their ranks: Neither shall one thrust another; they shall walk every one in his path."**

This characteristic of not breaking rank, of everyone marching in his own path, is both for our own sakes and for the sake of the body of Christ.

God has a plan for each person's life. Each individual life is a part of the whole, a piece of the great puzzle of His redemptive plan. But let us give heed to ourselves that we run our own course and do so very specifically. We must run the exact race that God has appointed us to run. In so doing we will be able to say with Paul, "I have finished my course..." [II Timothy 4:7]

Notice Paul said he had finished <u>his</u> course, not <u>a</u> course. Paul completed the specific race God had appointed him to run. His attitude of single mindedness and the clarity of vision he expressed in Philippians 3:13-14 is one that we would do well to adapt,

> **"Brethren, I count not myself to have apprehended: but this one thing I do, forgetting those things which are behind, and reaching forth unto those things which are before, I press toward the mark for the prize of the high calling of God in Christ Jesus."**

## Chapter Eleven

# Proper Balance in Spiritual Jurisdiction

### Being Brave to Man Your Post

Every truth and principle has a positive and a negative side. So far we have studied the boundaries which <u>limit</u> our authority of service. We have addressed the areas of caution that each person should take so not to violate his spiritual jurisdiction in the ministry. However, just as much as those borders define what we are <u>not</u> authorized to do, they also define the territory within which we <u>can</u> confidently operate as a ministry gift. In other words, our boundary lines define what we <u>can</u> do as much as what we cannot do.

For example, one that is called to pastor a local church must recognize the boundary lines outside which he should not go. This same man, however, must recognize that within his boundaries he must bravely take his place of ministry. A pastor not only has the commission and the responsibility, but also the authorization from God to protect and feed those sheep. He has the right to guard God's people because he has been commissioned to do so. He must not shrink back from his governing position. In I Peter, Peter told those who were responsible for the flock of God to, "take the oversight thereof." If a pastor does not take the spiritual oversight of a flock, the wolves will.

I believe that God is raising up brave pastors, both young and old, that will say, "No!", to Satan's wolf pack and not let them kill any more sheep with the poison of false doctrine and "Spiritual Fads". I believe that God is raising up pastors who will not be afraid to operate within the borders of their callings. Though they are fully aware of their limitations, they are also conscious of their responsibility and are bold within their calling to protect what belongs to the Lord.

Though we need to be aware of rights we do not have, we must be of a ready mind to accept those responsibilities that we have been given. Peter said that overseers must take the oversight, "not by constraint, but willingly." In other words, taking oversight of that which God has assigned to you should not be something you do begrudgingly, but something you do willingly and of a ready mind.

Peter went on to say, "Neither as being lords over God's heritage, but being examples to the flock." Here again is this issue of balance. You must take your rightful place, but you must take it the right way, for the right reason, and use the right method of operation. So do not be afraid to take your authority and rightful place in the ministry. Just be sure that it is truly your place and make sure you understand the purpose for your authority.

## A Right to Reap

In I Corinthians 9:1-14, Paul talked about yet another aspect of spiritual jurisdiction concerning rights to speak and rights of harvest. Though Paul was an apostle to the city of Corinth, evidently there were those who questioned his position of oversight in their church. Paul, however, quickly reminded them that they were the very offspring of his ministry. They were his children in the Lord, the very "seal of mine apostleship..." To those that did examine him, he stated that it was his labor that had given birth to their life with God, and that if anyone had a right to speak to them and to reap a harvest from them, he did. God's Word concerning spiritual jurisdiction teaches that a minister has a right to reap where they have sown. Note what Paul taught in I Corinthians 9:7,

> "Who goeth a warfare any time at his own charges?
> Who planteth a vineyard, and eateth not of the fruit
> thereof? Or who feedeth a flock, and eateth not of the
> milk of the flock."

Then in verse 11 he says,

> "If we have sown unto you spiritual things, is it a
> great thing if we shall reap your carnal things?"

A minister has a jurisdiction in the lives of those he has "given birth to" in the Lord. Not a right to lord it over them and dictate to them, but a right to speak, a right to reap, and a right to be respected in the Lord. Though one <u>does</u> have the right to reap where they have sown, the opposite is also true. One does <u>not</u> have the right to reap where they have <u>not</u> sown. This truth brings up a real problem that was not only prevalent in Paul's day, but also is in our day.

Many are attempting to reap a harvest where they have sown no seed. They are guilty of entering into other men's labors and stealing other men's sheep. In so doing they are transgressing both the law of spiritual jurisdiction and the law of love. There are even ministers that, for the sake of money, seduce younger ministers who are the fruit of another man's labors to follow them. It is sad when a spiritual father invests his life into a young minister and just about the time that the young man can be a blessing back to his spiritual father, another man comes along and literally steals the young minister away.

It is wrong for ministers to proselyte among another man's flock; especially the flock that consists of young ministers who are graduates of that man's Bible school. But it is also wrong for the younger ministers to follow that other man. If God has blessed you through a particular ministry or church, then you have a responsibility to reciprocate unto the laborer that blessed your life.

I see so many people violating this principle. For example, when they first begin to fellowship at a local church they may be financially broke, dumb to the Word of God and about to lose their whole family. After having been "put back together" by the ministry of that local church, just about the time they have reached the place where they can be a blessing back to that body, they move to another town or even to another church in that city. It is fine if God moves people, but having studied the responsibility of reciprocation, I do not believe God will move you till you have put something back into the place where you have been helped.

## Violators Will be Prosecuted

Transgressing the boundaries of another man's ministry jurisdiction is a very serious thing. We find cases in the Word of God where individuals were dealt with very harshly because of their failure to honor the boundary lines of another man's call. From early on in Biblical records we find those who wanted to lead a *"coup d'etat."* This word means, "a sudden overthrow of a government." In the body of Christ we would simply call this a church split. A split results when someone within the ranks of a ministry attempts to overthrow the present leadership and violates proper and ethical spiritual jurisdiction.

The first example of this recorded in God's Word is seen in Korah's rebellion in Numbers sixteen,

> "Now Korah...took men: And they rose up before Moses, with certain of the children of Israel, two hundred and fifty princes of the assembly, famous in the congregation, men of renown: And they gathered themselves together against Moses and against Aaron, and said unto them, Ye take too much upon you, seeing all the congregation of holy, every one of them, and the Lord is among them: wherefore then lift ye up yourselves above the congregation of the Lord? And when Moses heard it he fell upon his face: And he spake unto Korah and unto all his company, saying, Even tomorrow the Lord will shew who are his, and who is holy; and will cause him to come near unto him: even him whom he hath chosen will he cause to come near unto him. This do; Take censers, Korah, and all his company; And put fire therein, and put incense

in them before the Lord tomorrow: and it shall be that the man whom the Lord doth choose, he shall be holy: ye take to much upon you, ye sons of Levi. And Moses said unto Korah, Hear, I pray you, ye sons of Levi: Seemeth it but a small thing unto you, that the God of Israel hath separated you from the congregation of Israel, to bring you near to himself to do the service of the tabernacle of the Lord, and to stand before the congregation to minister unto them? And he hath brought thee near to him, and all thy brethren the sons of Levi with thee: and seek ye the priesthood also? For which cause both thou and all thy company are gathered together against the Lord: and what is Aaron, that ye murmur against him?"

**Numbers 16:1-11**

The result of Korah's insurrection was that he fell under the judgement of God and died with all his house and all his followers.

Overthrowing leadership is one of Satan's favorite tactics. He loves to divide and conquer. In fact, what Satan really did in heaven was lead an insurrection against the Lord and tried to take over. He deceived one third of the angels into believing that he could not only be like God, but that he could overthrow God. We read this of Satan in Isaiah 14:12-15,

"How art thou fallen from heaven, O Lucifer, son of the morning! how art thou cut down to the ground, which didst weaken the nations! For thou hast said in thine heart, I will ascend into heaven, I will exalt my throne above the stars of God: I will sit also upon the mount of the congregation, in the sides of the north: I will ascend above the heights of the clouds; I will be like the most High."

In reality, all Satan did was simply to go across town and start his own church with a third of God's congregation.

Violation of spiritual jurisdiction was not allowed to go unpunished with Satan, it was not allowed to go unpunished with Korah's rebellion against Moses, and God will have to

109

apologize to them if He allows individuals within the church to lead similar insurrections without judging them for their illegal activity.

In II Peter 2:10 God's Word says that more severely than His punishment of the unclean acts of homosexuality and the wickedness of Sodom and Gomorrah will be God's judgement upon those who, "...despise government. Presumptuous are they, selfwilled, they are not afraid to speak evil of dignities."

Paul, writing to young Timothy and speaking of "traitors" said,

> **"Now as Jannes and Jambres withstood Moses, so do these also resist the truth: men of corrupt minds, reprobate concerning the faith. But they shall proceed no further: for their folly shall be manifest unto all men, as their also was."**

Church splitting and proselyting from other pastor's flocks endangers both those who lead the wrong doing and those who follow.

Another area of violating spiritual jurisdiction and church splitting has been seen among those who call themselves apostles. I know of a church where the pastor specifically asked an "apostle" not to preach on a particular controversial topic. This false apostle willfully ignored the request of that pastor and, because of his selfwilledness, caused the church to split in half. Violations like this not only wreak havoc in the body of Christ, but hinder the moving of the Holy Spirit in our midst.

## Balancing Responsibility and Authority

We have learned that there are boundary lines which govern ministry, but we need to be careful that we keep a proper balance in our understanding and application of spiritual jurisdiction. One should not become so cautious in his approach that he does not take his rightful place of leadership. Others need to be careful as they take their place of authority that they remember what their authority is for. It is for serving, not ruling.

Jesus said in Matthew 23:11 that, "he that is greatest among you, shall be your servant." It is this "mind of Christ" of servanthood that Philippians 2:5-9 exhorts us to have in our life in the body of Christ.

Understanding the biblical purpose for authority and keeping it ever before your heart is the best safe guard against falling into an area of unbalanced application. Paul, in his teaching on the jurisdiction of his ministry in II Corinthians 10:8, shows us the purpose for authority,

> "For though I should boast somewhat more of our authority, which the Lord hath given us for your edification, and not for your destruction..."

Here we see that the purpose of authority is to edify and build up, not to tear down or destroy. The whole purpose of ministry is to serve and to help. In fact, in maintaining a proper perspective of authority, one should think more in terms of <u>responsibility</u> for and <u>stewardship</u> <u>of</u> that which belongs to God than of <u>rights</u> to enforce power. To think only in terms of authority will result in manipulation and control. To think in terms of responsibility and stewardship will result in a strong awareness of accountability to God and a faithfulness to serve.

In I Peter 5:1-4 the apostle Peter spoke of the need for those in spiritual authority to maintain a balanced perspective concerning their position of oversight. I Peter 5:1-4 says,

> "The elders which are among you I exhort, who am also an elder, and a witness of the sufferings of Christ, and also a partaker of the glory that shall be revealed: Feed the flock of God which is among you, taking the oversight thereof, not by constraint, but willingly, not for filthy lucre, but of a ready mind; Neither as being lords over God's heritage, but being ensamples to the flock. And when the chief Shepherd shall appear, ye shall receive a crown of glory that fadeth not away."

Notice the attitude of servitude and stewardship we should have in all areas of the ministry. We should think in terms of our responsibility to take care of that which belongs to God more than we think in terms of our authority or right to enforce power. There must, however, be a balance between these two points. Because God has given you the responsibility to serve, He has also given you the authority to carry out the task. Your authority, however, is for service, not for lordship.

# Chapter Twelve

# Conclusion

Through the God-given dream of Spiritual Jurisdiction, I began to realize why things happen the way they do and why many of the legal aspects of our redemption are not appropriated the way they are supposed to be. I understood for the first time why God's blessings, though promised in His Word, often go unappropriated by His children. I understood for the first time why Satan, though legally defeated through the work of Christ, still operates and often gains the victory over believers. I also understood for the first time the role and responsibility that we have to "work our own salvation"; doing our part by living within God's jurisdiction and out of Satan's reach.

This principle of Spiritual Jurisdiction encompasses and controls so much of our Christian walk. It governs our fellowship with God, our combat with the devil, and regulates our activity in the ministry. Spiritual Jurisdiction is truly a Pivotal Principle upon which many other laws hinge, and around which many other truths revolve.

This teaching on Spiritual Jurisdiction was not intended to magnify our limitations, however, but rather to emphasize ways to improve our effectiveness for God. Though this is a very serious and sobering message, it is exciting as well. For within the proper borders of our authority we can boldly fulfill the will of God!

God has given the church a divine mission. We have been entrusted with the awesome responsibility of *"occupying till He comes"* by preaching His gospel and demonstrating

Satan's defeat. For this reason we must diligently search out and then adhere to the laws that govern our spiritual authority and our individual ministries. I am confident that the more we cooperate with the laws of God, the more power, protection, and blessing we will experience.

I exhort you, therefore, to live to the fullness of your potential in life and ministry as you walk within the boundaries of your authority in God. I encourage you to maintain a "high altitude" in your walk with the Lord and fly high above the enemy that has been placed under your feet. As you do, you will enjoy the great benefits of the blessings of God and power over the enemy.

I trust that this study has shed new light on some already known truths. I believe that this message has articulated in a fresh way things that were already in your heart, but had not been clarified in a way that you could share them with others. I encourage you to share this book with others so that they, too, can walk in the fullness of their Spiritual Jurisdiction.

For additional copies of *Spiritual Jurisdiction* or more information concerning Mark's ministry write to:

**Mark Bishop Ministries**
P.O. Box 14121
Panama City Beach, Florida 32413